THE CENTER

THE

RADIO CITY

RADIO CITY

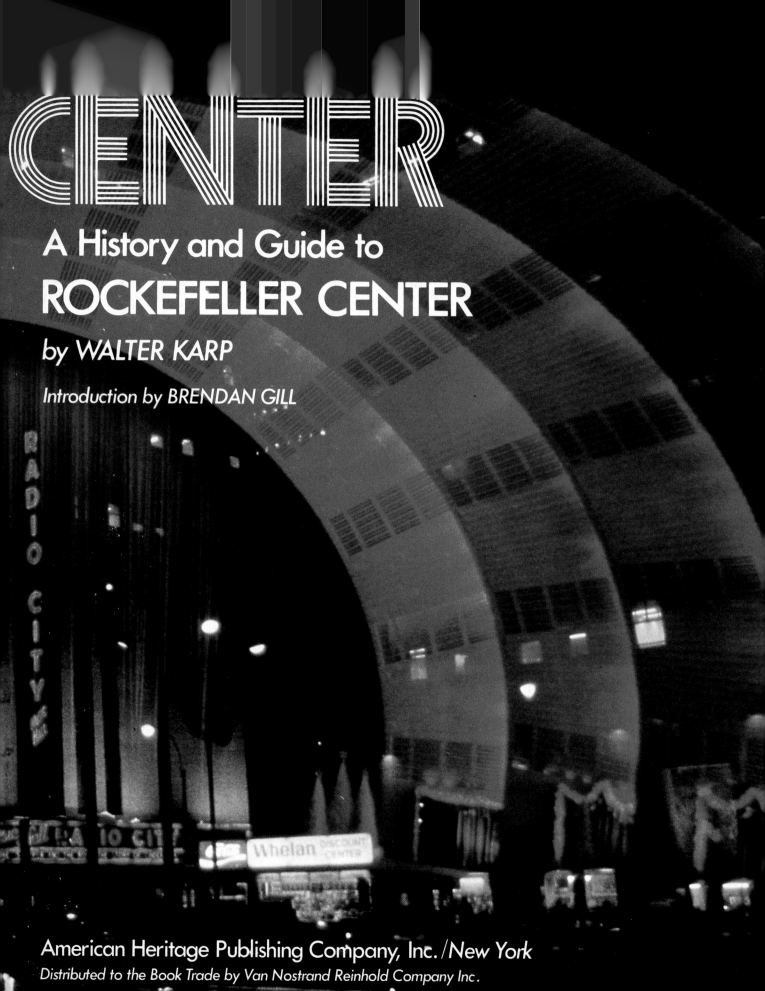

CENTER

A History and Guide to
ROCKEFELLER CENTER

by WALTER KARP

Introduction by BRENDAN GILL

American Heritage Publishing Company, Inc./New York

Distributed to the Book Trade by Van Nostrand Reinhold Company Inc.

CONTENTS

Manufactured in the United States of
America

Distributed to the Book Trade by
Van Nostrand Reinhold Company Inc.
135 West 50 Street, New York, N.Y.
10020

Karp, Walter.
  The center: a history and guide to
Rockefeller Center.

  Includes index.
  1. Rockefeller Center—Guide-books.
2. New York (N.Y.)—Buildings—Guide-
books. I. Title.
F128.8.R7K37 1982 ☒ 917.47'10443
☒ 82-18482 ISBN 0-442-24748-6

*Cover: Prometheus, the Titan of
Greek mythology who gave fire
to man, seems to float between
the Center's towers and its plaza
fountain.*
*Half title: Prometheus's precious
flame.*
*Back cover: Proscenium arch of
Radio City Music Hall, with
Rockettes imposed—precisely, as
always—above.*
*Opposite: Atlas, the Center's
other Titan, bears the world on
his shoulders.*

INTRODUCTION

The Center: The Heart of the City
by Brendan Gill

It is an odd fact of our local history that New York City from its earliest beginnings had not one heart but many. Yet if I were asked to name what is today the indisputable true heart of New York City, I would say at once that it is Rockefeller Center. Then I would add that the Center contains a heart within a heart; this innermost organ is the skating rink, which resembles its prototype not least in the degree to which it manifests ceaseless activity within a constricted space.

A casual visitor might assume that the existence of Rockefeller Center's prime location on Fifth Avenue was a stroke of luck. On the contrary, the ridge-straddling property survived as a consequence of generations of foresight. Because the landscape was comely and the distant prospects pleasing, the ground was chosen long ago as the site of a country estate, which later became an arboretum. For much the same reasons, the land just across Fifth Avenue was selected as the ideal plot upon which to erect St. Patrick's Cathedral. From the gentle eminence shared by Rockefeller Center and St. Patrick's, the land falls away on all sides. Once upon a time, one could look out from the crown of that eminence west to the Hudson River, east to the East River, south to the far-off, heavily built-up section of the city, and north to the quiet village of Harlem, dozing in its circle of orchards and pastures.

I call Rockefeller Center the true contemporary heart of New York, but I hasten to affix a proviso: that the heart is, in effect, a double one, with St. Patrick's and the Center dividing the honor between them. One portion of the heart is sacred and the other is, in the strict sense, profane, being devoted to commercial purposes; nevertheless, they complement each other without difficulty. New Yorkers claim them equally, with an innocent possessiveness happily remote from ownership. No matter what our personal religious beliefs may be, we feel free to wander at ease up and down the long twilit aisles of St. Patrick's, in very like the same fashion that we wander in bright sunlight up and down the Channel Gardens of the Center.

St. Patrick's was designed by a single architect, James Renwick, who revised and perfected his plans over several decades as the building rose against the sky. Most of Rockefeller Center was designed in haste, over a period of months, by a highly diverse team of architects. One isn't surprised at the aesthetic and structural integrity of the Cathedral, but how on earth did the many cooks at work upon the Center succeeded in not spoiling the broth? It is a feat of mingled inspiration and accommodation that architectural historians will go on pondering for as long as the Center stands, and what makes the feat all the more remarkable (and all the more mysterious) is the disparity between the projected future uses of the Center and the uses to which it was actually put. A critical factor in the design program was a subway that the city was planning to build on Sixth Avenue, following the demolition of the Sixth Avenue El. As things turned out, the El remained in place year after year until 1939 and the subway wasn't ready for operation until the early forties. The Center deftly adjusted itself to the delay, and Radio City Music Hall also adjusted itself to altered expectations. The skating rink was an inexpensive improvisation, not intended to last; today, nothing can challenge its zestful domination of the entire complex.

Certain individuals remain uncannily youthful as they advance in years, and there are buildings that enjoy the same fortunate privilege. Rockefeller Center amounts to an extended family of buildings, none of which, though they grow older, appears to grow old. I walk among them, remembering what it was to be young when they were young and envying them their imperviousness to the indignities of time. The designers of the buildings—Hood, Corbett, Fouilhoux, Stone, Harrison, and the rest (with whom I take pains to include that superb amateur architect, John D. Rockefeller, Jr.)—have long since laid down their pencils and T-squares, but sometimes, glancing into the bronze-gold duskiness of a shop window at the Center, I seem to surprise one or another of their benign ghosts standing beside me in shadowy reflection. Buildings are of stone, mortar, glass, and steel; they are also the sum of all the people who have lived in them, worked in them, and felt affection for them. The art of appreciating them consists of listening to what, all so silently, they have to tell us.

—Brendan Gill

St. Patrick's Cathedral in the 1930s faced deteriorated real estate owned by Columbia University. The dignity of the rising Rockefeller Center would complement the church.

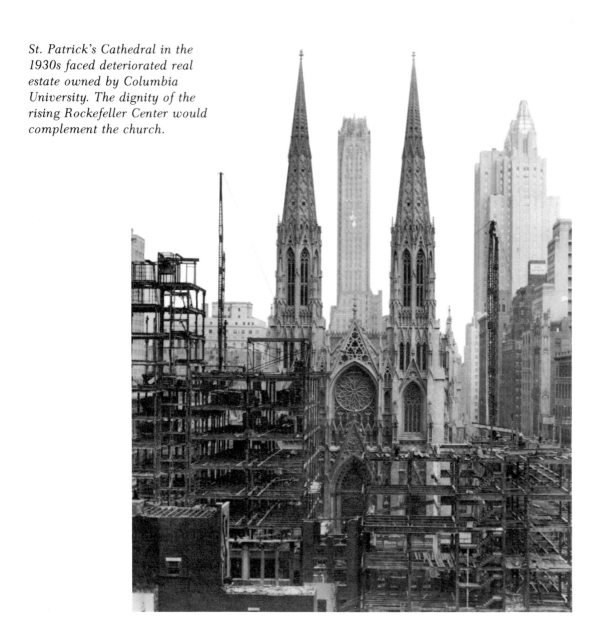

CHAPTER ONE
A Personality of Its Own

Raymond Hood, one of the architects who designed Rockefeller Center, imagined heaven-bound skyscrapers in a 1929 drawing (left).

EVERY YEAR more than fifty million people visit New York City's Rockefeller Center. They come for business, for pleasure, and, often enough, for both. No place on earth attracts more travelers than the "city-within-a-city" with its promenades and plazas, soaring office towers and underground shopping streets. Rockefeller Center is a place of business, yet it possesses an extraordinary power to please, to amuse, and to inspire affection. That power derives from no single feature, but rather from the fact that the Center comprises so many remarkably well blended yet contradictory features.

As Rockefeller Center opened its nineteenth building in 1973, the complex of skyscrapers still focused on the 70-story RCA Building, just as the original committee of architects had envisioned.

It is a place for laboring and a place for idling. It is a mighty urban development and it is also a welcome oasis in a particularly nerve-wracking city. It is commerce and entertainment; efficiency and art; power and gaiety. It is a place where elegant architecture manages to harmonize with ice skaters, garish umbrellas, and hot-dog stands on wheels. Inclusive, agreeable, ready to compromise, Rockefeller Center

The New York Times upheld John D. Rockefeller, Jr.'s status as an innovative multimillionaire with headline about his lease of Columbia's land.

is a testament to common sense. Built by one of the world's great private fortunes, it is uniquely democratic in spirit.

Interestingly enough, nobody planned it that way, not even John D. Rockefeller, Jr., the founder of Rockefeller Center and the final judge of everything that went into its making. The urban complex, which looks so carefully planned, is actually the product of clashing egos and unforeseen events, of opportunism and brilliant expediency, of boom-time optimism and depression despair. It was born to the sound of laughter and derision; and these, too, had a hand in its shaping. Rockefeller Center, in short, has a history, and perhaps the oddest thing about that history is that the two forces which made it all begin to happen are no longer operative or visible at the Center itself.

Force number one is Columbia University, which owns the land on which the original Center stands: substantially, the plot bounded on the south by West Forty-eighth Street, on the north by West Fifty-first

Columbia University, pictured below in 1828, still owns twelve of the original acres of Rockefeller Center land, as it has since 1814. Today the rent is some $12 million per year.

Street, on the east by Fifth Avenue, and on the west by Sixth Avenue (the Avenue of the Americas). In a city where land has been constantly divided and subdivided, the Columbia property was—and remains—one of the largest privately owned parcels of

The original scheme for the land leased by Mr. Rockefeller was to provide for a new Metropolitan Opera designed by architect Benjamin Morris which would face a square.

In 1932 speakeasies, sleazy boarding houses, and cheap shops filled the land opposite St. Patrick's. John D. Rockefeller, Jr., agreed to lease the space for $3.8 million a year.

land on New York's Manhattan Island. Had no such parcel existed, Rockefeller Center as it is today would not have been possible.

The second force is the world-famous Metropolitan Opera, whose ghost hovers over the Center at exactly the spot where the RCA Building now rises 850 triumphant feet above street level.

The history (or pre-history) of Rockefeller Center begins in January 1926, when the leaders of the Metropolitan Opera Company—chiefly multi-millionaire boxholders such as William K. Vanderbilt and J.P. Morgan—decided that their Opera House on Thirty-ninth Street and Broadway was no longer pleasing. In ever-changing New York, the once-fashionable Broadway neighborhood had become a squalid commercial district, and men who attended the Opera largely to display their limousines and their diamond-bedecked wives, thought the time had come to move grand opera "uptown"—the northerly direction in which fashionable New York had consistently been moving since even before the American Revolution.

In January 1928, after two years of vainly searching for a site, the Opera people were provided with a first-rate bit of real estate information. By what seemed a miraculous stroke of luck, almost all the leases on Columbia's midtown property were about

to fall due that very year. The property itself was a sordid mess. Once an ultrafashionable residential district, its 298 row houses were now largely boarding houses, night clubs, speakeasies, and bordellos. What was even more galling to the trustees of Columbia University, their twelve acres of prime New York real estate fetched Columbia only a wretched $300,000 a year in rents. Now Columbia sought to attract a few big commercial lessees, who would demolish the sleazy brownstones and transform the "Upper Estate" (as Columbia had called the property ever since getting it from the State of New York in 1814) into the richly productive property it had always promised to be. And what better way to attract such tenants than to have the prestigious "Met" become the first institution to adorn the site.

Columbia had good grounds for optimism in its financial expectations. Not only was the national economy riding high, but New York City was in the middle of the biggest and longest real estate boom in all its feverish history. The contagious optimism of an economic upsurge, the giddy feeling that anything is possible, was to color the views of most of the participants in the early history of Rockefeller Center, including Mr. Rockefeller himself.

The Opera group was as enthusiastic about the Columbia site as Columbia was about the Opera. No one was more enthusiastic or more influential than the Opera's personal architect, Benjamin Wistar Morris. A New York patrician, Morris envisioned a noble temple of grand opera rising on the central portion of the three-block Columbia prop-

erty. The building would face a large public square that would provide operagoers with the grandest of grand entrances. Columbia was so delighted with the idea it was even willing to break its basic rule of real estate holding and sell the land to the Opera outright. The only hitch was that the Opera did not, in fact, have available funds. Though backed by the high and the mighty, the Met traditionally limped along from season to season, perpetually losing money at the box office. By selling its property on Broadway, the Opera might be able to afford to pay Columbia the $3.8 million it was asking for the building site and to construct the Opera House. But the university also wanted $2.4 million

In 1859 the Rockefeller family home stood alone on Fifty-fourth Street north of where the Center would be built.

for the land on which the square would be developed, and this was quite beyond the Met's capacity.

Morris, however, was not dismayed. The money problem could be solved, he thought, not by moderating the plans but by making them even grander. These were boom times after all. Suppose, said Morris, that a "syndicate" of wealthy investors leased the *entire* Columbia property surrounding the future Opera House and square. With the latter as the lure, they could easily attract tenants willing to erect fashionable hotels and elegant department stores on the other three sides of the square. Since the success of such a huge undertaking rested on the prestige of the Opera, the syndicate members could "pay" for that prestige by themselves buying the land for the square and donating it as a gift to the city, thereby benefiting the syndicate, the tenants, the Metropolitan Opera, and the people of a city desperately short of public spaces. Morris himself drew up a breathtakingly elaborate scheme for the entire colossal development and unfurled it on May 21, 1928, at a dinner at New York's Metropolitan Club attended by some forty rich and mighty citizens.

"The thought is that this [plan] would make the square and the immediate surroundings the most valuable shopping district in the world." So reported Ivy Lee, the world's first "public relations" man, to his chief client, John D. Rockefeller, Jr., after hearing Morris speak at the dinner. At the time, Rockefeller was fifty-four years old, the only son and namesake of the aged founder of the Rockefeller fortune. "Mr. Jr.," as he was often referred to, had not been personally active in Rockefeller enterprises for years, preferring to devote his life and his wealth to an

The Elgin Botanic Garden was created by Dr. Hosack in 1801. It was a popular promenade area and a laboratory for herbs.

Dr. David Hosack, a physician and Columbia professor, owned the Center site from 1801 to 1811.

13

astonishing variety of philanthropic endeavors, including the restoration of Colonial Williamsburg, then in its initial stages.

The more Rockefeller thought about Morris's grand scheme the better he liked it. For one thing, as Rockefeller himself put it later, it was an "important civic improvement." Demolishing speakeasies to make room for grand opera must have been especially appealing to an ardent supporter of temperance. For another, it was a unique opportunity to develop a large parcel of land in a coherent and harmonious way, something that city planners had been advocating for decades in disorderly, chaotic New York. Moreover, it would provide an opportunity to demonstrate to all that a private real estate venture—one of the largest in history—could be both a profitable commercial undertaking and a beautiful civic amenity.

After vainly waiting two months for the so-called "syndicate" to form so that he could join it, Rockefeller decided to do what exceedingly few people in the world were rich enough to do. He decided to take the entire Opera House project under his own capacious wing. By August 1928, Rockefeller and Columbia University had reached agreement on their epoch-making real estate deal. Rockefeller agreed to lease the entire Upper Estate for twenty-four years at an average annual rental of $3.8 million, more than twelve times what Columbia was currently collecting in rents.

For Rockefeller, the lease meant a personal commitment of $91 million for the duration of the lease, plus tens of millions more in real estate taxes, a huge sum of money even in terms of the Rockefeller family fortune. The agreement gave Rockefeller the option to buy property in the central block for $3.6 million on condition that he sell it to the Opera for the same sum. He also had an option to buy land for "an open square" adjacent to the Opera site for the price of $2.4 million. This square Rockefeller intended to donate to the City of New York.

Before signing the contract, Rockefeller asked five real estate experts what they thought of his investment. All of them, recalled Rockefeller, "pronounced the project a sound one and good business." Such are the conceptions of men operating amid the delerium of a real estate boom. At this stage, Rockefeller had not the slightest notion that he himself would do any building. "I leased these three blocks never thinking for a moment but that I could shortly sublet the re-

maining property to various organizations which, without further investment on my part, would develop and finance their own buildings as the opera house proposed to do." What Rockefeller intended, presumably, was to assemble a team of architects and pay them what it would cost to perfect Morris's basic scheme for a luxury shopping district built round the Opera and its square. Once that was done New York's endless capacity for expansion and growth would take care of the rest. Speculative builders, hotelmen, and department store owners would flock to the Rockefeller offices, eager to sublet lots that fit neatly into a beautifully coordinated urban development.

If that thinking now sounds over-optimistic in these more prudent times, it should be judged in context. As Rockefeller's son Nelson explained years later, "It is a little difficult to recapture the flamboyant spirit of that era, when everything was going up: stock market, business, hopes, expectations, schemes, projects, everything." There was not a cloud in the sky on December 6, 1928 when Rockefeller organized the Metropolitan Square Corporation to handle the affairs of the project. Yet, exactly one year later, Rockefeller would find himself face to face with the prospect of a horrendous, humiliating fiasco.

First of all, the task of combining beauty and profit in urban design proved to be somewhat more difficult than anyone had supposed. It was one thing for the Metropolitan Square Corporation to invite architects to submit designs for the project. It was quite another to persuade them to take seriously the injunction to get an adequate return on the investment. Working from February to May, 1929, Rockefeller's Architectural Advisory Board (including Morris, Cass Gilbert, S.H. Bennett, and seven other prominent architects) showed little interest in making the development a self-sustaining enterprise.

To overcome this difficulty, Rockefeller's real estate adviser, Charles O. Heydt, made an important suggestion: Rockefeller should place the project's management in the iron grip of one John R. Todd, a tough-minded and enormously successful real estate developer who specialized in keeping architects under tight rein.

Far more serious was the frustrating indecisiveness of the Opera group. Instead of promptly putting up $3.6 million for their cherished site on the Columbia

*The communications
industries were the
first important
tenants in Rockefeller
Center, as this wall
relief commemorated.*

*On Tuesday, October 29, 1929,
anxious investors thronged Wall
Street as the stock market fell.
And the world changed forever,
Rockefeller Center along with it.*

The 102-stories-tall Empire State Building, completed in 1931, was a rival to the RCA Building in Rockefeller Center.

property, they kept coming to Rockefeller with a whole series of requests and demands. Chiefly they wanted him to pay the cost of buying out leaseholders who still encumbered the Opera's site. This was an expensive affair, since anyone who could obstruct the by-now famous "cultural center" (as the press billed it) expected to be paid dearly for getting out of the way. When the cost of lease-clearing reached $1.2 million, the Opera people asked Rockefeller to pay half the sum. Since Rockefeller was already giving the Opera a $2.4 million square, he declined to do so. To soften the rebuff, however, Rockefeller offered to lend the Opera $3.6 million on the easiest of terms. Even then the Opera board members refused to commit themselves to the project they themselves had inspired.

By August, the exasperated Heydt was convinced that the Met's leaders were deliberately foot-dragging in hopes of embarrassing Rockefeller into giving them a huge gift of money outright. "It is outrageous," Heydt wrote to his vacationing boss on August 19, "that the opera group should be playing us as they have."

As the Opera's plans grew more shadowy and its motives more open to question, there fell upon the entire national scene one of the most devastating blows in America history: the stock market crash of October 29, 1929—"Black Tuesday"—the day when the bottom began to drop out of New York's real estate market, including the market for the Opera's property on Thirty-ninth Street and Broadway. Financially hard-pressed in the best of times, the Metropolitan Opera Company was hapless in the crash. On December 6, 1929 New Yorkers read in their newspapers a stunning piece of news: "the project for locating the new opera house on the site offered by Mr. Rockefeller. . . has been abandoned," because of "difficulties" which were left discreetly unspecified.

The announcement did note, without further explanation, that Rockefeller would continue with the development. To the obvious question, what kind of development would it now be, the press gave no answer because Rockefeller had no answer to give. After being the much-lauded spearhead of the Opera

House project, he was momentarily nonplussed and not a little embarrassed. "With the Depression under way and values falling," Rockefeller later recalled, "I found myself committed to Columbia for a long-term lease utterly without the support of the enterprise by which and around which the whole development had been planned."

From the moment the Opera fell out of the project, its character was drastically altered. Except for the square, which was to be the Opera's permanent legacy to Rockefeller Center, the development had lost its civic and cultural object. It had become completely commercial. As one participant in the project said of the dark days of late 1929, "It was no longer a case of developing a 'cultural center' for the benefit of the Opera and the city, it was a case of finding a way to salvage the venture by any means possible."

Salvage was indeed the operative word, for the project's commercial prospects were grim. At a time when the vacancy rate for commercial space in midtown New York was rapidly increasing, at a time when the gigantic Empire State Building would soon open its doors for business, Rockefeller was proposing to add perhaps four million more square feet to an already glutted market. At a time when all major building construction was coming to a screeching halt around the country (builders do not build for glutted markets), Rockefeller was going to launch the largest urban commercial development in history. He was pitting one man's immense private fortune against the tidal force of a world-wide economic catastrophe. To make matters still worse, it soon became apparent that no prospective tenant was going to walk into the office of the Metropolitan Square Corporation, sublease a plot of land, and build his own building. Rockefeller would have to erect all the buildings himself or there was no hope of success whatever. The estimated cost of such construction was another $126 million, roughly a billion dollars in contemporary valuation.

There was but one way to avert disaster. Rockefeller would have to see to it that the commercial space he put on the glutted market was so superior to all rivals that prospective tenants, with

The Chrysler Building, completed in 1930, offered a futuristic, exotic style which Rockefeller architects avoided.

Webster Todd, left, and his father John, next to him, two of the managing team who controlled the construction, observe an early model with one building which would be called an oil can.

A Suggestion to Architects — By T. E. P

Cartoonists had a field day with the "oil can" building proposed for Rockefeller Center.

half of midtown to choose from, would chose the office space in his development. It would have to be outstanding in every conceivable way: in comfort and efficiency, cleanliness and service, engineering and layouts; in fresh air, light, and sparkling views. The development would have to have distinction, prestige, and an elegant-sounding address. The development would have to lure an abundance of passers-by and potential customers from Fifth Avenue for the new tenants' shops. Given the condition of the real estate market, Rockefeller and his associates had no choice but to strive for high quality. As John Todd rightly remarked, "Had we begun to build the kind of stuff that had been built in New York all during the 20's, we would probably have handed Mr. Rockefeller the biggest white elephant in all real estate history."

The truly awesome difficulty lay not so much in creating high quality, rentable space, but in creating *enough* of it to make the project a comercial success. A sufficient number of units had to be put on the market to generate the needed revenue; to neglect quantity would be fatal. On the other hand, to over-emphasize quantity in the designs could be equally fatal. Too many and too varied rental offerings would bring in congestion, inconvenience, and disorder. It would mean blocked views, menacing heights, and sunless streets that no one would care to walk through. To strike a balance between quantity and quality was obviously the key to success. But this meant juggling so many factors, making compromises among so many competing claims, that no single mind could have struck the balance. If Rockefeller Center represents "architecture by committee" it does so because it had to.

The team that now set out to perform this titanic balancing act had as its final judge and arbiter Rockefeller himself. It was he who gave final approval to all general policies as well as to all the architectural plans and ornamental designs. When the architects clashed, as they often did, "it was Mr. Rockefeller," noted his friend and biographer, Raymond Fosdick, "who acted as moderator in the ironing out of difficulties." The initial development of the project Rockefeller put into the hands of the sixty-two-year-old John Todd and four of Todd's associates (his brother James, his partner, Hugh Robertson, his son, Webster, and his son's partner, Joseph Brown). Their combined fee was $450,000 a year for six years, and they each bore the title of Managing Agent, but the undisputed boss was John R. Todd, an imperious, irritable man who looked like "an intelligent turtle," reported the *New Yorker*. He thought no day ill-spent if he could badger at least one architect into submission.

"Nobody in his right mind tried to argue with John R. Todd," one of the project's draftsmen recalled. The trick, he said, was learning "how to get around him" and around his definition of the architectural project as "an investment in real estate, the return for which must be in rented space."

In the winter of 1929-30 nobody dared challenge

The Center's architectural team worked under pressure with style. Raymond Hood, left, provided the grand inspiration, while Wallace Harrison, center, and Andrew Reinhard contributed talent and common sense.

Opposite: two of the 75,000 workers on the site toss a football across RCA girders.

Right: on the day after Christmas, 1933, St. Patrick's was photographed opposite the new foundation for the International Building.

Buildings Rise from Mud to Sky

Below: the first Rockefeller Center Christmas tree was an informal affair set up by workmen on the British Empire Building site in 1931. In the depths of the Depression workers line up for welcome pay on Christmas Eve.

21

Publicity played a part in turning public opinion in favor of the Center. Here workmen clown for the camera at dizzy heights.

Celebrities were lined up for the newsmen: Frances Perkins, State Commissioner of Labor in FDR's administration, dutifully watches a new drill.

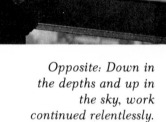

Opposite: Down in the depths and up in the sky, work continued relentlessly.

One of the two theaters is completed (below). Yet the Sixth Avenue El blights the Center's west boundary.

In keeping with the policy of windows and light for most inhabitants, the original fourteen buildings offered some 14,964 windows (photographed during construction of the Eastern Airlines Building in 1939).

Todd's ruthless practicality. A board of directors' resolution stated the matter clearly: "From now on the Square should be based upon a commercial center as beautiful as possible consistent with the maximum income that can be developed." With "maximum income" as their check rein (instead of the earlier, more easygoing hopes for a mere "reasonable financial return"), the architects associated with the project had precious little room to maneuver. Yet it subsequently became apparent that in the quest for balance between quantity and quality Todd's narrow pragmatism would require serious modification.

While the architects were working feverishly to come up with a "maximum income" design for the project, an extraordinary piece of luck came Rockefeller's way. An expansive new industrial empire, the Radio Corporation of America, let Rockefeller know that it was interested in stepping into the Opera's shoes as the principal tenant of the Rockefeller development. RCA controlled the National Broadcasting Company, with its two national networks and such popular radio programs as "Amos 'n' Andy," the Jack Benny Show, George Burns and Gracie Allen, and the Major Bowes "Amateur Hour." RCA also controlled Radio-Keith-Orpheum—RKO—one of the leading producers and exhibitors of motion pictures. It also owned RCA Victor, the leading manufacturer of phonographs. When serious negotiations began in February 1930 it was plain that the RCA empire could alter the entire character of Rockefeller's project. Not only did RCA want an enormous amount of prime office space, it also needed large facilities for its NBC studios and at least two spectacular RKO theaters on Sixth Avenue. For what he wanted, RCA's David Sarnoff was prepared to pay Rockefeller $4.25 million a year in rent.

In return for that enormous sum Rockefeller agreed to RCA's request that it be given the right to name the two theaters, to have its own name on a skyscraper, and to have that skyscraper occupy the central location in the development. RCA was also given the right to name that portion of the Rockefeller development which the RCA empire would occupy.

On June 4, 1930, news of the Rockefeller-RCA deal was announced to the press. It came as a considerable surprise. In the space of six months a plan for moving grand opera uptown had become a monument to mass entertainment. What had been a cultural center for the elite was to become, it seemed, an entertainment center for the masses, with "Amos 'n' Andy" supplanting *Aida* and the "talkies" supplanting ballet. It was to be called "Radio City" and the name captured the public imagination at once. In the deepening Depression it had a wonderfully heartening ring about it. Here, in midtown New York, would be the headquarters of modern technology and the new home of radio, the common man's friend. Science, Progress, and Democracy—such were the

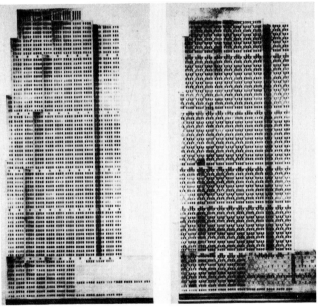

Alternate plans for the RCA Building included some by the brilliant Raymond Hood.

The Associated Press Building, completed in 1938, first modified the plan for the low flanking buildings.

*The RCA Building shows its
stepped-back design above the
Associated Press Building.*

powerful symbols which RCA's Radio City bestowed upon Rockefeller's projects—and Rockefeller wisely made the most of them. It is no coincidence that a Museum of Science and Industry would long occupy space at the Center, that the RCA Building's famed Rainbow Room would be a model of crystalline ultramodernity, or that "New Frontiers" would be the official theme of the Rockefeller Center art program. Of all the unforeseen events that shaped Rockefeller Center, few proved as influential as RCA's arrival on the scene.

The actual physical scene at that moment consisted chiefly of dust and rubble, as bulldozers in May 1930 began to bring to an end Columbia's portion of the midtown speakeasy belt. The only survivor was an unbudgeable "speak" on the northeast corner of Forty-ninth street and Sixth Avenue, which is open for business to this day—although the drinks, of course, are now legal. Clearing Columbia's site of its leaseholders was no laughing matter. By the time excavation began for Radio City (which would include the RCA Building, the RCA Building West, the RKO Building, the Radio City Music Hall, and a sister theater one block to the south), Rockefeller had spent several million dollars buying up the leases that still encumbered the Upper Estate. He had to spend millions more buying up the strip of land fronting Sixth Avenue, which Columbia had never owned. He had also taken out a $65 million mortgage with the Metropolitan Life Insurance Company at five percent interest. With rent, taxes, and interest, Rockefeller in 1931 was personally losing several million dollars a year. Even more ominous, by 1931 his development had lost the support of the public; for some time that loss seemed irreconcilable.

Trouble commenced on March 5, 1931 when the designers of the project revealed to the public a large plaster model of the latest design for the development. Until that day neither the public, the press, nor the critics had been given any real clue about what to expect. There had been tantalizing talk in the press about a great "entertainment center," still more pleasing talk about a Radio City and, most alluring of all, the prospect of a "city-within-a-city" taking shape in the midtown area. Just what all the talk actually portended nobody had any idea. That the Rockefeller development would be a profit-seeking commercial venture had not been made clear. No one had explained to the public and the press that, in Rockefeller's view, if the project were unprofitable it would be pointless. He believed that, if the Center did not produce dollars, its effect on society would be negative. Instead of serving as a model for other private developers to follow, it would be an object lesson in what to avoid. But the people, not understanding this philosophy and knowing only that Rockefeller's name had long been associated with large-scale philanthropy, took it for granted that his model project would be a utopian cityscape. It would be unlike the New York City of old, and it would be built with no regard for the cost.

What the press and the critics saw instead of that dream city on March 5 were five soaring office towers, a tiny square, and several fairly low buildings including a weird-looking, oval-shaped structure that was quickly likened to an oil can. The immediate response was savage fury intermixed with considerable bitterness. The *New York Herald Tribune* snarled its judgment: "The crux of the business is that Radio City is ugly. Its exterior is revoltingly dull and dreary." The *New York Times* complained of "architectural aberrations and monstrosities." Cartoonists did mocking sketches of "Oil Can City." Wits said the famous square was so small it would give visitors claustrophobia. Angry mail poured into newspapers around the country. The people at large felt betrayed. One more rich man, it seemed, had let them down badly. The ill will now felt toward the Rockefeller project proved remarkably intense and persistent.

When Rockefeller Center began suffering one financial setback after another, thereafter, the reversals aroused not sympathy but laughter and scorn. Disliked as a commercial venture, it was mocked as a commercial flop. One of the comedy highlights of the 1933 Broadway season was a skit in the musical review, *As Thousands Cheer*, which depicted John D. Rockefeller, Jr., vainly trying to get his canny old father to accept Rockefeller Center as a gift.

Every real estate expert in New York City expected the Center to fail, and to fail miserably. When RKO went bankrupt in 1933 and RCA itself began to totter financially, even Rockefeller, normally calm and detached, must have felt personally threatened and betrayed, first by the Opera people and now by the radio crowd.

Still, as Rockefeller himself remarked to Todd, there was no choice but to "keep sawing wood." On the rental front Rockefeller's management team began that spring to hunt for tenants in Europe, largely because they could find so few in America.

By October 1931 their efforts were crowned with success. A British syndicate agreed to lease one of two low buildings planned for Fifth Avenue and a French group agreed to rent its companion. Within the next few years Rockefeller Center's rental office would find itself deep in negotiations with half a dozen foreign countries, including the Soviet Union,

John D. Rockefeller, Jr., converses with Italian Senator Mosconi about the Palazzo d'Italia.

Nelson Rockefeller, twenty-four years old in 1935, headed the leasing program and offered prospective tenants inducements to settle in the Center.

with varying degrees of success. So, thanks to expedience, Rockefeller Center not only found prestigious tenants, it also acquired a second powerful theme to supplement the complex symbolism of Radio City—the theme of internationalism and international cooperation, which had long been dear to Rockefeller's heart. That theme's expression and monument

room was singularly quiet and determined, somehow imbued with a renewed purpose . . . . There seemed to be a little more appreciation, higher up, of what architecture meant after all."

It was in the aftermath of the "lambasting," as Todd called it, that the "oil can" building was supplanted by the two low buildings fronting on Fifth

With the Depression deepening, Mr. Rockefeller had trouble renting space in his new Center, so both American and European tenants were sought. In 1932 the cornerstone of the British Empire Building was laid by Lord Southborough (holding trowel) and Mr. Rockefeller.

would be a superb row of four low buildings fronting Fifth Avenue and a towering International Building set back from the street.

On the planning front the March public relations disaster left the architects convinced that major steps had to be taken to make the design more aesthetically pleasing. The time was ripe for "getting around Todd," as one draftsman, Walter Kilham, Jr., observed. "After all this abuse," he said, "the drafting

Avenue that would captivate the French and British investors. It was after the March blast, too, that the tiny square grew into a dramatic sunken plaza; that Raymond Hood, the most brilliant architect on the project, won approval for creating roof gardens on the building setbacks; that Todd was persuaded to use costly limestone (now a hallmark of the Center) instead of cost-cutting brick. By and large the Managing Agents proved amenable to the resurgent

Rockefeller Plaza is closed to traffic for twelve hours on one day each year in order to preserve its private status.

architects. As Hood remarked to a friend in August 1931, Todd is "the most conservative man in the world and every move we make is more and more modern."

Still and all, suspicion of architects was too deeply ingrained in the Todds not to burst out now and then. One day in 1931, for example, Hood suggested that the newly planned lower plaza be adorned with a large fountain. That was too much extravagance for Todd's brother James to bear. "Do you realize," he asked Hood, as if he were talking to a particularly dim-witted child, "how much it would cost per day to re-circulate 30,000 gallons of water?" "No, how much?" replied Hood. Todd thought for a moment and then answered: "Eight dollars and thirty cents." The fountain was installed.

By late 1931 the overall design of the Rockefeller

development was substantially completed. In the autumn of 1931 construction began on the RKO Building (now 1270 Avenue of the Americas) and the Radio City Music Hall. In January 1932 work began on the flagship of the entire project, the 70-story RCA Building. The next month the project at last acquired a proper name when Rockefeller was persuaded to put his own on the venture. On February 23, 1932 "Rockefeller Center" was officially born. In April the Metropolitan Square Corporation, Rockefeller's personal managerial instrument, became Rockefeller Center, Inc., thereby severing the remaining slender tie with the original Metropolitan Opera House plan. On December 27, 1932 the spectacular Music Hall opened its doors. In May 1933, the "Radio City" portion of Rockefeller Center was fully open and by July 1933 the international section was either complete or under construction. With some 75,000 workers at the site, the buildings went up with record speed.

Tentatively at first, people began poking around the novel-looking development and strolling on its new private street, which broke through New York's monotonous street pattern like a perpetually pleasant surprise. Although it was not even half-finished, the Center by 1934 was already beginning to demonstrate something of its power to please. Evidence that public opinion had begun to change drastically came in July 1934 when the producers of *As Thousands Cheer* decided to drop the Rockefeller skit from the show. It was no longer getting laughs, although not because the Center had become a financial success. Far from it. Despite attracting far more tenants than the real estate experts had dreamed possible, it was still losing some $3 million a year with no end to the operating deficits in sight. Audiences no longer laughed, because the Center had ceased to be a joke. As a critic put it in the November 1934 issue of *Architectural Forum*, the Center had become "an inspiring spectacle to New Yorkers and a respectable monument to Mr. Rockefeller."

The commercial project, derided and jeered at for nearly three years, was slowly but surely asserting its dignity, its amiability, and its founder's deep sincerity of purpose. If, as John Todd remarked, the Center's success depended on its having "a personality of its own," then, despite the red ink in the ledger books, Rockefeller Center was well on its way to success.

In December 1936 another brilliant stroke of expedience added the finishing touch to the Center's developing personality. The crowning stroke came about, ironically, because of a failure in the commercial planning. The luxury shops that lined the sunken

The sunken plaza in its early stages was intended to be an entrance to the underground shops.

plaza were failing to attract customers and had to be replaced by two restaurants. These, in turn, required the closing of two entrances that led from the plaza to the Center's undergound streets. With that the lower plaza had lost its commercial function of welcoming customers, and nobody could figure out what to do about it. Then one day a Cleveland inventor named M.C. Carpenter asked Rockefeller Center Inc. if it would let him test out his new-fangled artificial ice-skating rink. The management was ready to try anything. On Christmas Day, 1936, purely as a temporary stopgap, ice-skating commenced in Rockefeller Center. It was an instant and overwhelming success; the uniqueness of the Center was highlighted. There was something wonderfully exhilarating about gliding around so freely in the very heart of

Rockefeller Plaza, the private street which distinguishes the Center, under construction.

a commercial development; it was entrancing just to watch the skaters gliding and curvetting on the ice.

With the coming of ice-skating to the sunken plaza, Rockefeller Center had truly achieved a "personality of its own." It had evolved into an entity strong enough to triumph over the Great Depression: an efficient place of business with the power to give pleasure to multitudes. The Center's management, now led by young Nelson Rockefeller, knew a good innovation when they saw one. In 1939 permanent machinery was installed for the skating pond, which provides more innocent merriment for more people than any other spot in New York City.

The year 1939 was a fitting date for making ice-skating a permanent feature of Rockefeller Center. For that year, in a gala ceremony in November, John D. Rockefeller, Jr., drove the "last rivet" into the fourteenth and last building of Rockefeller Center. Eleven years had passed since "Mr. Jr." had initially agreed to lease Columbia's Upper Estate for a hefty boom-time price. The long ordeal was now over. At the cost of some $100 million in construction, rent, and taxes, the Center was all but complete, or so Rockefeller himself believed. Henceforth the expansion of the Center would have to take place well beyond the boundaries of Columbia's Upper Estate whose lease still bore his name. Henceforth, the Center's destiny would be largely in the hands of his sons. John D. Jr.'s Center was, in truth, complete.

The further expansion of Rockefeller Center was

The new Time & Life Building, capped with a Christmas tree.

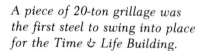

A piece of 20-ton grillage was the first steel to swing into place for the Time & Life Building.

part of no plan. It was largely a response to practical necessity. The chief factor in the expansion was, quite simply, the internal expansion of corporate tenants who outgrew their original quarters in the Center. The earliest example of this occurred within five years of the "last rivet" ceremony when Esso—Standard Oil of New Jersey—informed Rockefeller Center's management that it needed far more room than it had. Since the Center, which had finally begun to show an operating profit in 1941, was fully rented, Esso, it seemed, had no choice but to move out of Rockefeller Center's spaces into a new building of its own.

In the short run that would have done the Center no harm whatever. There were any number of tenants clamoring to take Esso's place. Rockefeller Center, however, had not been built for the short run. From the very start it was meant to be not only a success but a lasting one. To allow Esso, a "family" tenant, to bid the Center goodbye might be interpreted by gimlet-eyed realtors as the first sign that the Center's status was beginning to slip. Although John

The Time & Life Building demonstrated Rockefeller Center's determination to hold on to its clients. The building itself, finished in 1959, was carefully designed to fit the city's needs and to pass the tests of weather machines.

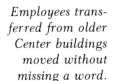

Employees transferred from older Center buildings moved without missing a word.

D. Rockefeller, Jr., had no desire to expand his Center, he understood what the situation demanded. In July 1944 he approved plans for postwar construction of a 33-story building on Fifty-first Street due north of Rockefeller Plaza. The bounds of the Upper Estate were now definitely broken.

The Esso lesson was not lost on Laurance Rockefeller, John D.'s son, who became Chairman of the Board of Rockefeller Center, Inc. in 1951. In order to provide against another such emergency, he began assembling property on the west side of Sixth Avenue. The avenue, though known since 1945 as the Avenue of the Americas, was still as seedy as it had been in the days when the speakeasies bloomed and

an ugly elevated railroad rumbled along its sunless length. A long-range vision of the future was necessary to imagine that anything like a clean and modern city could one day develop here.

Laurance Rockefeller's foresight was soon reward-ed. In the mid-1950s Time Inc., one of the most famous tenants in Rockefeller Center, decided it, too, had outgrown its accommodations at the Center. Even more potentially damaging to the Center's hard-earned prestige was the fact that the famed magazine publishing house was thinking of erecting its own new building on Park Avenue, a fashionable residential district which was then being trans-formed into a new center of sleekly modernistic glass

The walk-through waterfall in the McGraw-Hill Park is a whimsical element in the new public spaces west of Sixth Avenue.

Exxon Park, completed in 1971, continues a Center tradition of public spaces which are oases in the grid pattern of the city.

In 1973 the "Sun Triangle," which is positioned to show the relationship of Sun and Earth at solar noon in New York, was installed in the McGraw-Hill Building's sunken plaza.

skyscrapers. People might well conclude from such a move that the Center, once the very symbol of Progress and the Future, was becoming dim and passé.

Determined not to let this happen, the Center's managers, after prolonged negotiating, finally persuaded Time Inc. to remain on Rockefeller property, if not in the original Center itself. The result was the first leap across Sixth Avenue to the seedy side of the street. In December 1959, the Time & Life Building was opened on a somewhat awkward angle to the rest of Rockefeller Center. When the founder of

Rockefeller Center died the following year at the ripe old age of eighty-six, the Center once again seemed complete, if a little lopsided. Once again it found cause to expand.

Curiously enough, it was Esso which again supplied the impetus. By 1963 the huge company—now known as Exxon—had outgrown even its new building. Since Exxon was quite content to move across the avenue and stand shoulder to shoulder with Time & Life, Center officials saw an opportunity to restore physical coherence to Rockefeller

Center. Rockefeller Center, Inc. began silently buying up three blocks' worth of property along Sixth Avenue south of the Time & Life Building. The idea was to erect not only a new tower for Exxon, but two more soaring buildings to the south of it. Like the Time & Life Building, each of the three new buildings would feature an attractive plaza in the front, the whole monumental row forming what one architectural writer has termed "a coordinated architectural complex with the old Center across the street." Completed in 1973, this western half of the enlarged Rockefeller Center is physically linked to the older eastern half by superb underground pedestrian malls. Spiritually it is linked to it by sharing the Center's enduring policy of providing both for the needs of its tenants and for the convenience and amusement of the public at large.

But one thing was assuredly different. Whereas the task of designing the original Rockefeller development had been an awesome pioneering undertaking, the erection of the expanded Center was merely the working out of what had already been demonstrated as a hugely successful urban concept.

A four-block-long series of plazas turned Sixth Avenue into an urban sculpture garden.

"Cubed Curve" by William Crovello embellishes the Time & Life Building plaza.

An enormous real estate venture, such as the building of Rockefeller Center, needs subtle and extended public relations if it is to succeed. The first image of the building created in drawings and models before it is erected, is as important as it will ever be afterward. John Wenrich's drawings served this purpose of introducing the Center to the world.

The idea of the city in the America of the late 1920s and early 1930s was riding a crest that had been swelling ever since the population began to move off the farm, in pursuit of the wages and security of industry, shortly after the Civil War. City lights mingled with stars atop the awesome skyscrapers which began to rise around the turn of the century. When John D. Rockefeller, Jr., set out to build his "city-within-a-city" in 1931, after the Metropolitan Opera backed out of a commitment to serve as a centerpiece, he wanted to make the nascent Rockefeller Center appeal to both the general public and potential corporate tenants.

The first model of the Center, shown to the press and critics on

Looking northeast with St. Patrick's in the upper right: the RCA Building is garlanded with the proposed roof gardens for the Center, including a botanical observatory.

An aerial view looking west across the Hudson, right, shows Rockefeller Center as John Wenrich imagined it in all its golden glory. The city, with all the glamour of modern design, would triumph over the hard Depression realities.

The Center's sunken plaza, as envisioned by Wenrich in 1932, boasted a grandiose fountain (but not the statue of Prometheus that now commands the scene), plus shops and entrances to the Concourse (rather than today's restaurants). Nor could the artist foresee the plaza's most notable feature: the skating rink which has brought so much life and color to this vital space just off Fifth Avenue.

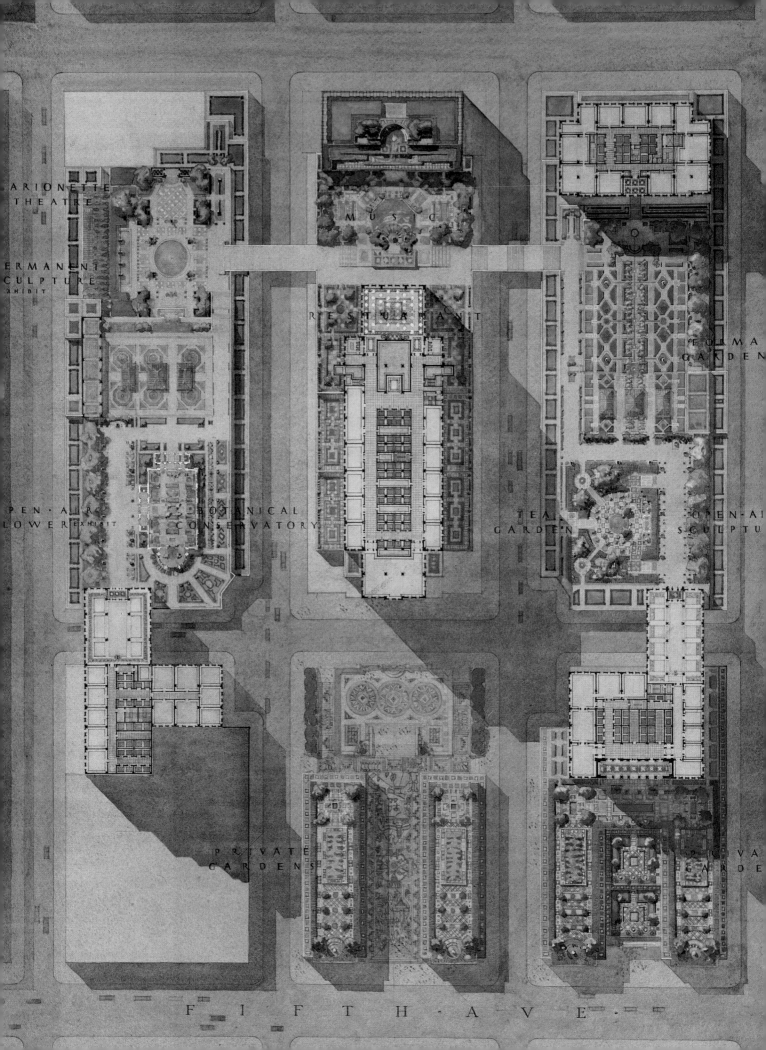

MARIONETTE THEATRE

PERMANENT SCULPTURE EXHIBIT

MUSIC

RESTUARANT

OPEN AIR FLOWER EXHIBIT

BOTANICAL CONSERVATORY

FORMAL GARDEN

TEA GARDEN

OPEN AIR SCULPTURE

PRIVATE GARDENS

PRIVATE GARDEN

FIFTH · AVE ·

March 5, 1931, provoked violently hostile reactions. According to the *New York Herald Tribune*, "the crux of the business is that Radio City is ugly. Its exterior is revoltingly dull and dreary." A small oval structure proposed for Fifth Avenue was referred to as an "oil can," making a snide reference to the source of the Rockefeller fortune. The managers of Rockefeller Center were taken aback by the public reaction and realized they would have to think out their plans better and present them more handsomely. The revised thinking of the architectural committee was realized in drawings—called "renderings" in architectural parlance— which the architects could use to convince the managers of the worth of their plan and the manager could in turn use to persuade the public.

There were two men working on renderings of Rockefeller Center. One of these was Hugh Ferriss, a prominent architect who had turned to making visionary renderings of other architects' plans, the other was John Wenrich. Ferriss set the tone of silvery towers rising into the sky with romantic and mysterious canyons at their base, but he left the project early on. John Wenrich, whose career may have peaked with his work on Rockefeller Center, stayed to create the definitive picture of what the Center should become and did become for many people.

Wenrich's solid but graceful shafts rise in steps like Mayan pyramids from urbanely decorated bases. His center square is populated with shadowy civilized figures who lounge and promenade as though they have found a secret respite from the bustlings of the greater city around them. For images of strength and power, modulated by style, the Center buildings, as Wenrich presented them, had no peers in 1935 and have been challenged by few since.

The eagle's-eye view opposite is from a point above the RCA Building. It shows the roof gardens planned for the Center.

Looking due west along Forty-ninth Street: John Wenrich's vision of the RCA Building was designed to rekindle the soaring image New York had of itself before the Crash.

"Time"—the giant mural covering the ceiling of the RCA Building lobby—typifies the art glorifying the Center as a "machine-age temple."

CHAPTER TWO
Useful and Noble Halls

WHEN ROCKEFELLER'S TEAM of architects was instructed to plan a "commercial center" around a "square" that would bring in "the maximum income," it was presented with a problem in architectural design with few parallels from the past as a guide. This is because "maximum income" in New York meant tall buildings and these had always before been designed as individual projects. Nobody had ever been asked to design several of them at once as part of a planned and integrated complex of commercial buildings, let alone on a scale as huge as the future Rockefeller Center. The architectural group that began its post-Opera exertions in December 1929 had to feel its way through considerable darkness.

Fortunately for the success of Rockefeller Center, Rockefeller and Todd had chosen their team well. The members, informally called the "Associated Architects," were alike enough to be able to work together, yet different enough to ensure that every problem would generate a variety of design solutions for Rockefeller to choose from.

To make certain that his own brand of practicality would be strongly represented, Todd hired two of his former architectural employees, L. Andrew Reinhard and his partner, Henry Hofmeister. Their chief merit in Todd's eyes was that "they had worked with us before on our theory that in business property income production supercedes pure aesthetics." Unlike virtually every other successful New York architect, Reinhard and Hofmeister were not silver-spoon gentlemen who had completed their architectural training with a sojourn at the famed Ecole des Beaux-Arts in Paris. Reinhard, for one, was the son of a carpenter who began his architectural career as a fourteen-year-old clerk in the office of Benjamin Morris. Unlike most successful architects, too,

Public square and private street made the heart of the Center unique. Plans for circular and oval designs were considered for the square.

Reinhard and Hofmeister did not regard a corporate client as a patron of the arts whose money was to be lavishly spent. On the contrary, these two modern and well-trained architects regarded such a client as a businessman who had hired them to use his money wisely and profitably.

Todd recognized, however, that such a complex

imaginative, Hood was one architect on the Rockefeller project who knew how to "get around" Todd. He was able to do this partly because he was genuinely charming and still more because he could usually find a commercial reason for proposals that were essentially "aesthetic." Hood was to be the most influential architect on the design team until

This pre-1938 photo shows the lower plaza as pure open space. A summer restaurant and winter skating in the plaza now comprise the Center's pièce de résistance.

project should not be based on only one philosophy, even if that philosophical viewpoint happened to be his own. That was one strong reason for the presence on the architectural team of the ebullient Raymond Hood, described in a *New Yorker* profile as "the brilliant bad boy" of architecture. Hood was a Beaux-Arts graduate who, unlike his suave fellow alumni, delighted in wearing unorthodox clothes and talking in passionate and colorful language. More important, he was a master hand at designing bold and dramatic skyscrapers. Earthy, zestful, and

his untimely death in 1934 at the age of fifty-three.

In sharp contrast to Hood, though equally eminent professionally, was Harvey Wiley Corbett, another alumnus of the Ecole des Beaux-Arts. The fifty-six-year-old Corbett was an elegant man-about-town who wore dress gloves and carried his walking stick into the drafting room. Todd said he liked Corbett because he had "a mind open to the modern trend," in other words, because he would bring a third point of view to the project. Moreover, Corbett was deeply interested in matters of direct concern to

A time-exposure photograph
lighted by a 30-second stop at
each floor illumines the 800-foot
shaft of an RCA Building elevator, looking upward. Elevator
banks were at the core of the
building so that most offices had
windows—an innovation in 1932.

Rockefeller Center's overall design, such as studying
ways to segregate automobiles from pedestrian traffic, and exploring the use of multilevel arcades and
promenades to form physical links between towering buildings and so integrate them into a larger urban design.

Unfortunately, Corbett never really thrived under
the conditions of architecture-by-committee. It took
considerable toughness of character to see one's
ideas being constantly torn to pieces—often by the
hectoring Todd—without losing faith in one's abil-
ity to contribute. There was nothing relaxed or easy-

*Elegant marble floors
and inviting murals
surround the RCA
Building elevators.*

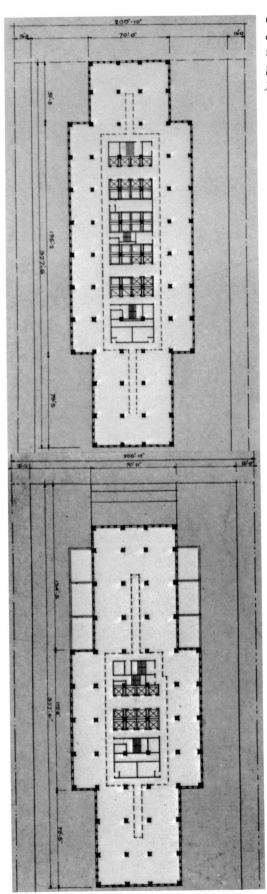

going about the designing of Rockefeller Center. Office discipline was rigid; architectural draftsmen worked in serried ranks like so many clerks in an insurance company. The architects not only clashed with each other and with Todd, they often had to stand by while their handiwork was picked apart by a whole battery of non-architects. As Reinhard explained the design process, even "a very desirable layout" would have to pass muster with "the rental agent" who used his "long experience with tenants" to criticize the design. It would then be examined by the builder who would "show where costs can be reduced by a change here and there." Then it would go to the engineer who might "point out the difficulties in electrical service or framing." From there it would pass to the lawyers, who would judge whether the plan conformed to the tenant's lease or to the complicated requirements of New York's municipal ordinances. As Corbett's junior partner, Wallace K. Harrison, recalled many years later, working on the architectural team "could be awful" at times.

For Harrison, however, it proved to be the opportunity of a lifetime. At thirty-four the youngest member of the group, he was destined to become, after Hood, Rockefeller Center's most important architect and decades later, the chief designer of the "new" Center across the Avenue of the Americas. He, too, was a Beaux-Arts graduate, and the Center architect most devoted to simple clean-cut geometrical forms, a style still looked upon in 1929 as "wild modernism" by the irrepressible Todd.

Despite their clashes with the Managing Agents, the leading architects in the group shared with Todd an important principle of building design: that one worked, in Todd's words, "from the inside out." In Harrison's formulation of the same principle, the design objective was to "fit the buildings to the activities, needs and comforts of the workers in them." Hood, too, claimed that his "chief architectural theory is to build buildings for those who live in them rather than for those who are to see them from the street."

These architectural dicta are often given the gen-

eral name of "functionalism," the assertion that the outward form of a building should "express," in architectural jargon, the chief human and mechanical activities carried on within them. In the design of office buildings this often meant no more than the notion that the needs of the tenants —the paying customers—were the only thing that really mattered. The functionalist credo would play an important part in the creation of Rockefeller Center, but it was not the guiding principle. How could it be, when the basic "need" of many of the paying tenants—shopkeepers and department stores—was to have an endless parade of pedestrians trooping by their show windows? How could the functionalist credo dominate when even corporate tenants housed on the fortieth floor wanted —and could demand—a lively and animated work place? In Rockefeller Center "those who are to see ... from the street" were crucial to the success of the Center; equally important were the tenants who occupied the buildings.

Functionalism, in and of itself, was incapable of solving the quintessential problem facing the Associated Architects. Rockefeller had handed them a twelve-acre parcel of land that stretched from prestigious Fifth Avenue to delapidated Sixth Avenue, a long and discouraging 900 feet away. The question was, how might the new development persuade people who were perfectly content to stroll along Fifth Avenue to head westward to the heart of midtown seediness?

Whatever else Rockefeller Center would be, what it had to offer first and foremost was a *magnet* powerful enough to pull people off a pleasant avenue into the midst of a pile of commercial buildings. Why should they want to leave Fifth? The architects had to give them a compelling reason. What could lure them toward Sixth? The architects had to design the lure.

Here is where the original "square," first set aside

GENERAL DYNAMICS BUILDING

IT'S CARNIVAL TIME

SAVINGS

Whelan DISCOUNT CENTER

Coca-Cola

Garage attendants used firemen's poles in the 800-car garage.

Marble lobbies are buffed at night for the tenants' convenience.

Behind the scenes: Men and Machines

The Indiana limestone covering the RCA façade is cleaned on the Sixth Avenue side, opposite. Careful maintenance and a gray serenity distinguish Rockefeller Center buildings.

Handsome 1938 sedans filled the first underground garage in a New York office building.

As it was perfected, air conditioning was installed to cool the Center.

A staff of nearly 900 work regularly to keep the Center sparkling.

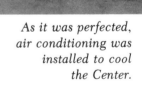

Special elevated platforms raised by electricity facilitated the cleaning of high windows.

A mural of photomontage scenes from the Center enlivened the former Headquarters reception area.

The Center's numerous roof gardens brought urbanity to urban architecture.

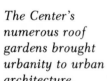

Thousands of office windows in the Center are cleaned by workers in rotation. From his vantage point this worker also watched the St. Patrick's Day Parade.

Night shift crews from the Electrical Division change lights so that none ever need be out.

Rockefeller Center developed a special nozzle attachment to clean the blue steel blinds which complemented the gray limestone exteriors.

53

*The ramp built to
divert delivery trucks was part
of the sophisticated traffic
control.*

for the central block, became the key to the entire design. Usable public spaces were something New Yorkers needed badly. To the footsore, the nerve-wracked, and the preoccupied (which in midtown Manhattan means practically everybody), the attraction of these spaces is great. That attraction, however, did not automatically solve the architects' problem, for the attraction was purely potential. A city square could be a barren and repellent place. In New York City today there are numerous plazas fronting skyscrapers which are so cold and uninviting their chief habitués are pigeons. On the other hand, cozy little squares in congested New York can be so overwhelmed by the tall buildings around them that anyone sitting in one feels as if great walls are about to fall in on him. New York City has plenty of failed or passed-by areas for congregation—or exploitation.

It was in avoiding both pitfalls that the Beaux-Arts training of Corbett, Hood, and Harrison eventually paid handsome dividends. At the Paris school,

*The plans for the underground
delivery station showed
many levels.*

SHIPPING PLATFORM FOR R.C.A BLDG

UNDERGROUND TRUCKING AREA

MACHINE ROOM

A 50TH STREET RAMP ENTRANCE

B TO R.C.A BUILDING
TO BRITISH EMPIRE BLDG.
TO LA MAISON FRANCAISE

C TO BUILDINGS NOW UNDER CONSTRUCTION.

TRAFFIC RAMP ROCKEFELLER CENTER NEW YORK CITY N.Y.

*The timeless idiom of the
Center's design contrasts with
these trucks which seemed modern
in the 1930s.*

which was founded in 1793, symmetry was regarded as the indispensable attribute of every noble architectural design. Moreover, the kind of symmetry which the school deemed desirable was "axial," meaning that all the elements in the design were balanced on each side of a central dividing line or axis. This axis was usually treated as a long, dramatic vista at the end of which stood some dominating point of interest. In Rockefeller Center, that point was to have been supplied by the Opera House. In the first post-Opera plans, that vital spot retained its Beaux-Arts funtion. It was designated "main building no. 1"—the future site of the RCA Building.

With a skyscraper in line with it, the square at once became an important element in a larger axial design. It was no longer just a dead space in midtown. To fulfill its function as a magnet, what the plaza needed next was some kind of link to Fifth Avenue that would complete the axis. A walkway from the avenue to the square would not only complete the formal axis, it would also serve to funnel people into the heart of the Center, Beaux-Arts form serving a commercial function.

Interestingly, designing that funnel proved to be a trying problem for the Associated Architects. In several plans the passageway actually resembled a funnel, since the walkway to the square consisted of the hollowed-out ground floor, or arcade, of a large building fronting Fifth Avenue. An alternative idea was the one that appeared in the plan that was "lambasted" in March 1931. In this plan the lower level arcade has completely disappeared. In its place appears a squat oval building on Fifth Avenue, the cartoonists' "oil can." The aesthetic idea behind the oval shape was that people walking along Fifth Avenue would have difficulty passing a curved building without hugging its walls until they were drawn into the middle of the development.

What lay behind these inept designs was ,perhaps, a too-literal devotion to "maximum income." Since Fifth Avenue shops paid very high rents, Todd, for one, was loath to waste too much Fifth Avenue frontage on a mere pedestrian promenade. The logic of the Beaux-Arts axis was too strong to be denied, however. The much-criticized "oil can" was quickly replaced by the two low buildings so positioned that they formed the shop-lined flanks of a sloping pedestrian promenade leading to the future lower plaza. Eventually the whole would form a long dramatic vista from Fifth Avenue to the majestic upsurge of the RCA Building, which is set off not only by a sunken plaza but by a private street as well.

That street is an excellent example of how random, even ephemeral factors helped produce some of the finest features of Rockefeller Center. The purpose of the private street, according to Hood, was to "obtain the maximum ... street perimeter" for the Center's future department stores. Since Rockefeller Center never did succeed in attracting a major department store, the extra street has achieved little of its original commercial purpose. Yet it has done something far more important. The very presence of a special street, boldly contrasting with New York's monotonous street pattern, has done more to make the Center seem a special precinct, a true city-within-a-city, than any other single element in the complex design.

In creating the overall design, the plan for the central block turned out to be a marriage between the axial principles of Beaux-Arts design and the commercial principle of maximum return on investment. In working out plans for the north and south blocks, however, the combination of maximum income and the New York Zoning Resolution had more influence than any of the architectural refinements.

Promulgated back in 1916, the zoning rules had among their objectives the desire to stop New York's newer commercial streets from being turned into sunless canyons like the streets in the old Wall Street area. The regulations were also intended to prevent any one skyscraper builder from blotting out a neighboring skyscraper's light and air. Under the complicated rules, a person could build on every inch of his property up to the height of 100 feet. Beyond that the building had to cover less than the full space, in accordance with certain specified formulas. In other words, an architect's New York building had to become narrower. Only if you, the client, built on one fourth of your property were you and your architect free to go as high as you wanted without any further narrowing.

Even during the giddy real estate boom nobody did anything so foolish as to use only a fourth of his property. With prospective tenants ready to snap up every square foot of new commercial space, architects were told to design huge, bulky structures which went along with the minimum amount of narrowing required by the zoning rules. This minimal narrowing was accomplished by means of a graduated series of setbacks which made post-1916 New York skyscrapers look like enormous many-tiered wedding cakes.

The Rockefeller Center architects spurned the "wedding cake" style of the 1920s for the eminently practical reason that broad bulky buildings included a great deal of interior space far from windows, and in 1930 the chances of renting such dimly

lighted space was nearly nil. The best way for the architects to observe the zoning laws and also construct the maximum amount of *rentable* space would be to build a number of 100-foot buildings on the north and south blocks of the Center. By building low over a large portion of each block Rockefeller gained the right, under the city's Zoning Resolution, to build at least two very tall straight buildings on each of these blocks. Keeping the skyscrapers well apart from each other, Hood explained in the January 1932 issue of *Architectural Forum*, produced a "staggered tower plan like a five-spot card"—the fifth "spot" being the centrally located tower of the RCA Building. "In the towers," continued Hood, "is concentrated office space, which is thus as ideal as possible since every office has a

International tenants were sought for shops as well as offices.

potential outside view and light. In the lower part, i.e., below the 100-foot level, are concentrated theaters, stores and all those retail spaces that require direct contact with the street and can be artificially lighted and ventilated."

This basic design plan was to lead to some notable advances in the art of high-rise construction. These advances were first worked out in detail for

poorly ventilated, dimly lit interiors are unappealing even in the best of circumstances. As Todd once remarked, he had never made an extra dollar of rental on space that was 30 feet or more from a window. What he meant was that such space commanded so little rent it did little more than pay for the cost of constructing it. In the Great Depression there was no point in putting such space on the glut-

Corporate logos such as those displayed here complemented the Center's high-style commerce.

The Center offered shoppers a variety of consumer goods.

the RCA Building, "main building no. 1," the tallest and finest of all the office towers in Rockefeller Center, now as well as then.

The essential principle of the RCA design was a rule of thumb long known to New York builders: daylight in the latitude of New York City can penetrate the interior of buildings to a distance of roughly 27 feet. Space located more than that distance away from a window will require artificial lighting even on a clear afternoon. As office space,

ted market. Instead, the Associated Architects were asked to design the RCA Building (and other buildings as well) in such a way that every floor above the broad base level would provide never more than 27½ feet of depth inside a window wall. This was a novel idea and it led at once to another.

In order to conform to the new 27½-foot rule, the architects hit upon a design technique that has been followed ever since by architects and builders. They decided to concentrate all the elevator banks and building utilities in the dim central portion of the building, the unrentable interior space. Surrounding this core would be the building's main corridors, and surrounding these would be office spaces exactly 27½ feet wide from window to corridor. It was to be no small part of Rockefeller Center's appeal to tenants that even their humblest clerks had an ample share of natural light to work in. Strictly commercial calculations, modified by Depression conditions, made Rockefeller Center a notably humane place to work.

In the design of Rockefeller Center one thing often led to another. The decision to sell no unappealing space led to the 27½-foot rule; that rule led to the idea of a central utilities core; the sum of all three led to the possibility of constructing a towering building that was also extremely slender for most of its height. This presented a daring new look in skyscrapers, and Hood was determined to make the most of its dramatic possibilities. So, too, were his architectural colleagues, though they argued heatedly about what was to be done.

To Harrison, the most progressive of the Associated Architects, the 27½-foot rule meant a golden opportunity to build a slab-like building, one in which every vestige of the old "wedding cake" look would be entirely eliminated. It would rise up sheer without a single distracting indentation to mar its stark geometry. In the early 1930s such a building would have been strikingly new and widely acclaimed by the more modern-minded school of architects. Moreover, it would be quite economical because setbacks are costly to build. Since the RCA Building would be so slender, the Zoning Resolution required no setbacks in the tower portion. Why not dispense with them entirely? Reinhard and Hofmeister weighed in on the side of Harrison, which strongly suggests that Todd did so as well.

Hood stood out against the others. He insisted that the RCA Building be given small, delicate-looking setbacks at three different levels of the 70-story building. He wanted to create, on the east, or Fifth Avenue, side of the building a facade that consisted of an extremely narrow central shaft flanked by two stepped-back wings even more slender still. What he sought to create was a tower which, when seen from Fifth Avenue, would look as if it were not only soaring skyward but gently receding as it soared. It was a thoroughly poetic conception, replete with roof gardens and artistic detailing. Since poetic arguments made very little

impact on John R. Todd in 1930, the ever-resourceful Hood offered a purely practical argument for his dramatic scheme.

The setbacks, he insisted, would be entirely functional. They would each occur at a point where one of the RCA Building's elevator banks came to an end. Since each subtraction of an elevator bank might add a bit of dark interior space to the floor plan and since the architects were directed to

Originally, the RCA Building lobby was more commodious and practical than glamorous and artful. This view from the mid-1930s shows the lobby before the installation of the famous Sert mural, the dramatic lighting, and the broad and welcoming information desk.

eliminate such space, his narrow setbacks would reduce the floor area precisely in accordance with the 27½-foot rule.

The fine pragmatic ring to Hood's argument could scarely disguise the gaping hole in it. Compared to the cost of constructing setbacks hundreds of feet above the ground, the amount of interior office space that would be eliminated was so minisscule it was economically meaningless. Hood surely understood this well but he needed the gambit for his game with Todd. By observing the prescribed rule with slavish fidelity, he made it difficult for Todd to disagree with him—even though such fidelity was economically absurd. On the other hand, had he said what he really felt, Todd could have hooted him down with ease; for what Hood wanted to achieve was a building that was not only eminently rentable, but one that would be thrilling

to behold, like the spire of a cathedral or the prow of a majestic steamship.

This does not mean that Hood was more "aesthetic" and less "practical" than his colleagues. It would be truer to say that he was more imaginatively practical than they. He simply grasped more clearly than they did that the RCA Building had to be the visual focus of the entire Center. Standing at the end of the axis leading from Fifth Avenue, it had

to stop Fifth Avenue pedestrians in their tracks by the sheer dramatic force of its presence. Only then could a promenade and a square have a chance to pull them into the midst of the Rockefeller development. Since Rockefeller himself was the final arbiter of serious clashes between the architects, it is safe to say that he understood Hood's real intentions quite well, for, ultimately, Hood's solution prevailed.

Architectural disputes notwithstanding, when the Radio Corporation of America became the chief tenant of "main building no. 1," it was obvious to everyone that the tower had to be made into the Center's focal point within as well as without. This was partly because RCA planned to house the radio studios of the National Broadcasting Company in a special ten-story segment of the new skyscraper. The studios and the radio stars were bound to attract enormous crowds, for in the quagmire of the Depression Americans were strongly attached to radio (with an intensity that television, child of prosperity, was never able to arouse). Knowing this, the Center's architects took pains to design the building so that it would express, with maximum force and clarity, the democratic spirit of Rockefeller Center.

That spirit is most strongly marked in the design of the RCA Building's lobby, which stands in sharp contrast to the lobbies of the great majority of luxury commercial buildings. In the latter, lobbies are deliberately meant to be spectacular, overwhelmingly displays, usually designed to impress the visitor with the wealth and majesty of the building's principal corporate tenant. The RCA Building lobby is not like that at all. It is not ornate; it is not spectacular. It is designed not to overwhelm but to welcome. Taking advantage of the building's great length and its centralized grouping of elevator banks, the designers turned the lobby into an internal pedestrian mall, a place to stroll through, with the two long parallel aisles serving as inviting promenades. The sense of being welcomed is fortified by innumerable design details: by the broadness of the lobby's corridors, which suggests a public rather than a private space; by the handsome yet eminently sturdy flooring, which suggests an interior sidewalk; by the broad commodious staircases, by the wide, friendly brass handrails, and by the neat, sensible store fronts. The hospitable, egalitarian spirit of the RCA Building cannot be duplicated anywhere in the realm of commercial buildings and in precious few public buildings, either.

The architects were not only determined to make

the RCA Building an attraction, they also wanted to use it to integrate all of the Center's buildings into a single unified system. For a time the "Radio City" aspect of the Center threatened to envelop the entire design plan, as the architects tried out one imaginative design after another for unifying the Center physically. In the end they were able to accomplish a high degree of unification with their decision to install a large underground shopping street below the RCA Building lobby and to link this to all the other future buildings of the Center. The resulting Concourse, as it is called, eventually became a "city-beneath-the-city" which, from the start, lent a certain other-worldly enchantment to Rockefeller Center. It also compelled the architects to decide once and for all what the exact form of the square would be.

During nearly two years of designing Rockefeller Center this question had not been dealt with. The Opera's legacy to Rockefeller's project kept changing its size and shape almost every time a new version of the overall design (there were dozens) was given to the draftsmen to set down in detail. At one time or another it had been positioned above ground, then at ground level. It had been broad and it had been narrow, rectangular and oval. These

alterations and hesitations reflected the vital importance of the square and the architects' determination not to decide too hastily its ultimate form. After two years of intense concentration they finally produced a masterpiece by committing a major mistake, thereby supplying another example of the ironic side of the Rockefeller Center story.

The blunder came about after the architects had definitely decided to create an underground street system for Rockefeller Center. Having made this decision, the next step, obviously, was to guarantee that the shop-lined Concourse would be filled with people. Although every building would provide an entrance to the underground world—the access in the International Building is part of a majestic bank of escalators—these were considered insufficient, for the great number of looked-for shoppers. Just who thought of turning the square into a sunken foyer for the Concourse is not known for certain. The idea itself was bold, dramatic, and highly original. Here, along the grand axis of the Center, would be the visible sign that the Center not only existed above ground but had a second alluring life below it. The sloping Promenade would carry people to the eastern edge of this dramatically sunken space. From there a grand staircase would bring them to the plaza floor, whence Hood's fountain would lure them toward the western wall of the plaza. At that point two sets of doors, one on each side of the fountain, would bring them into the underground world. The commercial purpose of all this is obvious. Unless the Concourse supplied its shops with customers, no retailer would rent one.

The idea never worked. The sunken plaza, as it was first known, attracted lively throngs to the heart of the Center, but it did not lure them down the staircase. Visitors were more than content to tarry around the periphery of the plaza, to sit on its benches, or stroll along its terraces and look at the Center buildings around them. They saw little reason to descend the staircase and open the doors to the Concourse.

The architects had miscalculated; and, with the advantage of hindsight, it is easy to see where they went wrong. They had created a dramatic space, strategically situated between the garden-bedecked Promenade and a majestic office tower. They had provided, at the edge of the plaza, the finest view in the Center—the point where most of the complicated pieces of the design fell firmly into place.

Sculptor Rene Chambellan's bronze Tritons and Nereids frolic in the fountains of the Channel Gardens Promenade.

Moreover, they had equipped it, by the very nature of their design, with a precious patch of open sky, a rarity in midtown Manhattan. Having created so singularly pleasant a place to tarry (for which they deserve full credit) the architects neglected to ask themselves the next question: why, except in a rainstorm, would people wish to exchange that for an underground street with no view? The very features that made the sunken plaza a popular success was what doomed it as a conduit for commerce. Like its companion, the private street, Rockefeller Center's world-famous lower plaza is the triumphant result of initial miscalculation.

Mistake or not, the creation of the sunken plaza, which was opened in early 1932, marked the completion of the basic design of Rockefeller Center. Although most of the individual buildings had not yet been planned, the RCA Building had set the stan-

dard that was to be applied to the others. The 27½-foot rule would remain a basic construction principle until the Associated Press insisted in 1937 that it could use a broad bulky building with plenty of dim interior space. The exterior treatment of the RCA Building—the use of limestone and the placement and decoration of the windows—would be re-

The last piece of
limestone was lifted
into place on the
RCA building
in 1932.

The gothic style of
the RCA observation
tower pleased Mr.
Rockefeller.

The roof gardens on
the low buildings
were an imaginative
inspiration of
Raymond Hood.

peated in other buildings. So, too, would various materials and motifs first chosen for the interior of the RCA Building.

Two pressure-packed years of designing and the rough give-and-take of the design process strongly affected the participants. In the course of making complex compromises everybody had to surrender a portion of his private stock of cherished attitudes, ideas, and preconceptions, most notably John R. Todd. Determined in December 1929 to scotch any "purely aesthetic" extravagance, he slowly but surely came to realize that there was far more to the Center's brand of commercial success than he had imagined in his long and unfailingly successful career in real estate. By 1932 Todd was ordering his protégé, Henry Hofmeister, *not* to neglect aesthetic values in planning the 41-story International Building. "Keep back far enough if you can from Fifth Avenue with your tower so that you retain the beauty, charm and light of the Italian and German buildings" he instructed Hofmeister. "It will not do just to build square buildings with straight fronts." It sounded as though Todd had learned a thing or two from the leadership of Raymond Hood, just as Hood had learned much from Todd. Doubtless everyone learned something from everyone else and the Center was the ultimate beneficiary of the molding and harmonizing of so many talents, viewpoints, and tastes. It is precisely because the designers took so much into account that the Center's appeal is both broad and enduring.

Concerning one aspect of the Center's design, however, there was no need to work out a complicated compromise. After the 1931 critical assault everyone concerned with the project was convinced that a large-scale program of decorative embellishment was absolutely essential to the ultimate success of the Center. What the architects, in particular, had in mind were carved reliefs for the Center's numerous doorways, decorative panels and plaques for the exterior walls, large muted murals for the lobby of the RCA Building, and a few larger-than-life sculptures for the most strategic sites in the development. Rockefeller agreed to set aside some

Rockefeller Center art follows a symbolic style. Leo Friedlander's sculpture represents "Television."

Artist Diego Rivera, the noted Mexican Communist, created a mural which was destroyed because it was thought too radical.

Ezra Winter stands before the mural "Fountain of Youth" which he painted for Radio City Music Hall.

$150,000 for the art program, a huge sum in the Depression. More than thirty artists were to be commissioned to adorn Rockefeller Center, including the Mexican Marxist Diego Rivera who created a sensation when he worked a portrait of Lenin into an RCA Building mural. The artists produced more than 100 major works of art as well as scores of minor decorative devices. They were done in a wide variety of materials including wood, stone, and bronze and such tradition-breaking media as stainless steel, aluminum, and cast glass. The art program of Rockefeller Center constitutes a veritable indoor and outdoor museum of 1930s art, but you often have to look up to appreciate it.

Behind the unanimous support for an expensive and inherently troublesome art program lay a number of urgent reasons, or reasons which certainly seemed urgent in 1931. For one thing, it was hoped that an elaborate program of artistic embellishment would go far to please the general public, some of

Sculptor Lee Lawrie, opposite, views "Wisdom," his limestone creation above the RCA Building entrance. An awesome image was wanted.

whom had felt betrayed when the commercial nature of Rockefeller Center was first brought home to them. Secondly, the art program was intended to explain to the public the meaning and significance of the Center through the symbolic power of art. Lastly, the art work was intended to make the modern and functional buildings look less severe and the Center more cheerful. Since the Center would turn out to be a notably amiable place, it is clear that the art program's urgency stemmed in part from the architects' inability to believe how extraordinarily attractive and delightful their own handiwork would be. That disbelief is perhaps understandable. In 1931, the Center, as a physical entity, consisted of one giant hole in the ground and the beginnings of a small forest of rising steel girders. The future Center looked so grim that as late as 1933, with the RCA Building already complete, one architectural

critic freely predicted that the Center would become a "necropolis," a city of the dead.

In any case, the art program was launched in earnest when one Hartley Burr Alexander, professor of philosophy at the University of Southern California, was commissioned to develop a theme for the Center. It was to sum up what the Center signified and thereby supply the art program with a related set of ideas for the artists to depict or symbolize. Professor Alexander tackled his assignment with a laudable exuberance of spirit. He not only devised and expatiated at length on a number of possible grand themes—"Man the Maker" was his first; "The Frontiers of Time" would be his last—he took it upon himself to concoct richly suggestive and elaborately detailed topics for the artists to represent. For the most important entrance to the Center, the Rockefeller Plaza doorway to the RCA

A metal and enamel plaque on Radio City Music Hall symbolizes "Song."

To represent an eternal concept of intelligence, artists used the antique medium of mosaic.

The latest word in Art Deco was an aluminum statue by Robert Laurent, recalling the Leda myth.

Building, Professor Alexander proposed the general notion of a "Voice Speaking Through Time and Space" and suggested further that the panel north of the "Voice" symbolize Light and the southern panel symbolize Sound and that the whole be done in glass for brilliancy of effect. He produced entire scenarios for such abstruse subjects as "Intelligence Awakening the Public," "Genius Seizing the Light of the Sun," and "The Gifts of the Earth to Mankind."

Professor Alexander's general themes held no appeal for the builders; he returned to California leaving no direct influence on the artists who would follow. Eventually Rockefeller Center officials announced that the art program's theme would be "New Frontiers and the March of Civilization." Still, Professor Alexander's vigorous efforts had not gone to waste. The artists chosen by a blue-ribbon Art Advisory Committee carried out some of Alexander's suggestions with remarkable fidelity. Alexander's "Voice" became the sculptor Lee Lawrie's "Wisdom" which was created in several tons of glass and stone for the RCA Building entrance, just

as Alexander had suggested, and which duly includes a north panel symbolizing Light and a south panel symbolizing Sound. Similarly, the professor's "Intelligence Awakening the Public" became (with "mankind" substituted for "the public") Barry Faulkner's mosaic frieze decorating the Sixth Avenue entrance to the RCA Building West.

Even though Professor Alexander's scenarios did not directly apply, his taste for grand abstractions and cosmic themes set the tone to a certain extent for much of the art program. Thus, Prometheus, the firebearer (by Paul Manship), glistens in the lower plaza while his brother Titan, Atlas, bearer of the world (by Lee Lawrie), forever flexes bronze muscles across the avenue from St. Patrick's Cathedral. In the art program as ultimately carried out, only Rockefeller's deep personal devotion to international themes counterbalanced Professor Alexander's passion for cosmic myths and symbols.

Just what effect the art program has had upon the public is hard to determine. Aside from the murals and the two famous Titans and Rene Chambellan's

In 1965 bronze panels by Giacomo Manzu replaced art taken from the Palazzo d'Italia in 1940.

fine bronze fountainheads in the Channel Gardens of the Promenade, many of the carvings, reliefs, screens, and plaques are above eye level and rarely attract the unobservant eye. They are more sensed than felt. Were they to disappear overnight their absence would surely be noticed, though few visitors

Pedestrians pause and reflect before "Intelligence Awakening Mankind."

This mosaic was crafted by Italian workers from more than one million pieces of enamel.

José María Sert, conservative Spanish painter, inspects his RCA lobby mural.

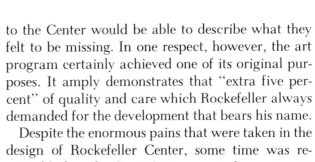

to the Center would be able to describe what they felt to be missing. In one respect, however, the art program certainly achieved one of its original purposes. It amply demonstrates that "extra five percent" of quality and care which Rockefeller always demanded for the development that bears his name.

Despite the enormous pains that were taken in the design of Rockefeller Center, some time was required before the Center's true merits began to win critical appreciation. The first critic to offer praise, however, was none less than one of the greatest ar-

"American Progress"
by Sert yearns across
the RCA Building
lobby.

A primal female, reflecting sen-
timents of the period, is sculpted
by Gwen Lux.

chitectural thinkers of the twentieth century, the
famed Frenchman, Le Corbusier, who visited
Rockefeller Center in 1936 and came away enthralled by what he saw. Here, as he later informed
his countrymen, was nothing less than the
"machine-age temple." It "affirms to the world the
dignity of the new times by its useful and noble
halls," said Corbusier, thereby vindicating Rockefeller's basic—and savagely derided—decision to
make his huge development a model of modern urban life rather than a utopian alternative to it. In
Corbusier's view, that business-like decision had
more to do with the Center's importance than did
the work of the architects themselves. Architects
"rush in with their heads down," said Corbusier;

thanks to Rockefeller's decision "they are launched on the paths of the modern spirit." The builders of the Center were creating a rational new skyscraper style, not by theorizing in solitude, but by coming to grips with soaring land values, with urban density, with the needs of giant corporations, and with the relentless demands of commerce—"the formidable internal pressure which mobilizes their efforts," as Corbusier rightly put it. It was the modern world, operating through Rockefeller and Todd, Hood and Harrison, through builders, engineers, and the real estate market, which had ultimately produced the Center's "useful and noble halls."

The public did not deeply ponder, as Corbusier did, the meaning of Rockefeller Center, but Americans delighted in it as much as he did and perhaps for some of the very same reasons. Why did the

Influential architect and critic Le Corbusier took delighted interest in the buildings of Rockefeller Center.

"What makes the Center architecturally the most exciting mass of buildings in the city is the nearby view of the play of mass against mass, of low structures against high ones, of the blank walls of the theaters against the vast checkered slabs of glass in the new garage. . . Rockefeller Center has turned into an impressive collection of structures."
—Lewis Mumford
The New Yorker, May 4, 1940

Center so "excite the popular imagination" asked Frederick Lewis Allen, the famed social historian, in the October 1938 issue of *Harper's Magazine*. Because "this is the Future ... embodied in actual stone and steel for all to see; the future of engineering marvels and efficiency and air-conditioned comfort." That was not all, said Allen. "These buildings are not simply huge, efficient, and comfortable.

They are also gay." The lower plaza on a warm afternoon, he said, was like "a shipboard scene, full of animation, and sunlight, and a sense of holiday." What the Center portended for the "Future," Allen confessed he did not know. "Meanwhile," he advised his readers, "we may at least enjoy its splendor, its color and its abounding life." And people have been doing just that for half a century.

Portfolio: The Art of Rockefeller Center

Late in 1931, $150,000—a huge sum in the Depression—was set aside to embellish the lobbies, doorways, the Promenade, and the square of Rockefeller Center with artwork. Equally importantly, Hartley Burr Alexander, professor of philosophy at the University of Southern California, was hired as a consultant to develop a "theme for Rockefeller City."

Professor Alexander made several suggestions, including "The Frontiers of Time," which were received with only lukewarm enthusiasm. Subsequently, Mr. Rockefeller consulted a committee of conservative academics, and from all the suggestions he received the theme "New Frontiers and the March of Civilization" was wrought. The combination of commerce and idealism seemed almost Victorian, but the art produced was pure 1930s in style. Ultimately, some of the specific thematic proposals Professor Alexander had made were incorporated in the Center's art, his voice being one among many.

There are more than one hundred works of art created by thirty artists in various locations throughout the Center. Lee Lawrie's "Atlas" holding an open sphere of the world stands in front of the International Building, opposite the portals of St. Patrick's; a companion Titan, "Prometheus," disports himself hugely across the fountain wall of the sunken plaza (a location for which "Atlas" may have been intended). A masterpiece which exemplifies one of Professor Alexander's themes is the Jovian sculpture of "Wisdom" above the main entrance to the RCA Building.

In such a work as the mural "Fountain of Youth," by Ezra Winter, in the main lobby of the Radio City Music Hall, the symbolic details so specifically follow Professor Alexander's scenario that it is somewhat difficult to interpret the painting on its own. On the other hand, Isamu Noguchi's stainless steel bas-relief "News," over the entrance to the Associated Press Building, is a powerful combination of sculpted forms which stands on its own.

One commission which was not happily fulfilled went to the Mexican muralist Diego Rivera, who was prominently Marxist. His controversial painting of "Man at the Crossroads . . . Looking to a New and Better Future" contained a portrait of Lenin; it was replaced by "American Progress," a mural painted by Spanish conservative José María Sert.

Much of the Center's art exists high above the public's heads as they walk by, and it may not be part of many people's daily experience. But

The limestone screen fronting the International Building, sculpted by Lee Lawrie in 1935, depicts the history of humanity in fifteen polychrome panels. Lee Lawrie directs work on the massive allegory: inserts top, center, bottom left. Insert top right: an early version of the RKO Building lobby contained a Boardman Robinson mural exalting humanity's moral values; center: Isamu Noguchi burnishes his plaque for the AP Building; bottom: Lawrie's Atlas assembled.

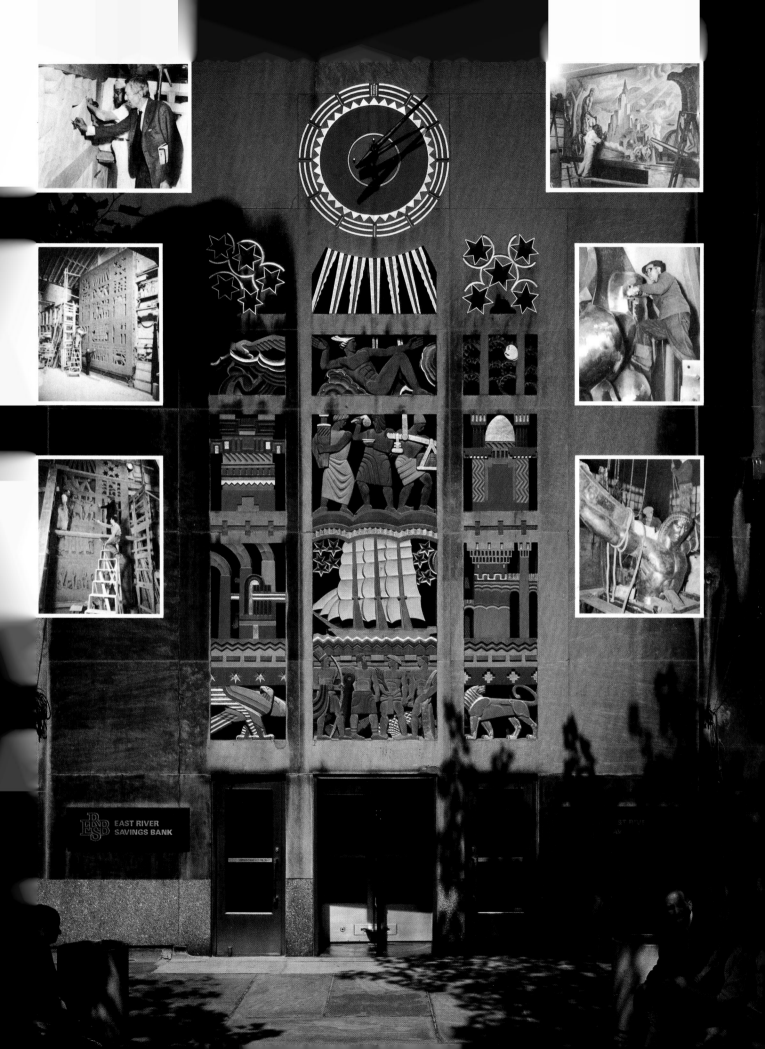

EAST RIVER
SAVINGS BANK

The rooftop
gardens of
Rockefeller Center
recall the lush
elegance of
the architects'
original plans.

"Wisdom and
knowledge shall be
the stability of thy
times," a text from
Isaiah, with central
figure cut from lime-
stone, by sculptor Lee
Lawrie, greets visitors
to the RCA Building.

Gaston Lachaise's
bas-relief panel,
one of four created
in 1933, antici-
pated the benefits
of modern civiliza-
tion—even the
conquest of space.

The hastening fig-
ure of Mercury,
representing com-
merce, flashes in
gold upon the
façade of the
British Empire
Building.

Above the entrance to 14 West Forty-ninth Street, a panel by Lee Lawrie symbolizes progress and inspiration.

Glowering on the wall of the British Empire Building: three non-traditional lions.

With Rockefeller Center rising in the background, José María Sert's mural in the main lobby of the RCA Building demonstrates how the Muses (at right) and the forces of action including Abraham Lincoln (at left) complement each other in creating "American Progress."

The well-known passage from Isaiah proposing world peace was crafted in limestone by Lee Lawrie for the entrance to 19 West Fiftieth Street.

Passing 1270 Avenue of the Americas, a horse and hansom cab appear to frighten Pegasus on the south façade.

the stylistic integrity, the wide experimentation in media, and the superior quality of the craftsmanship lend Rockefeller Center a distinction which gives a new lustre to the ancient ideal of urban art.

With the march of Rockefeller Center across the Avenue of the Americas—which continues to be known colloquially to most New Yorkers as Sixth Avenue—new concepts of urban design had to be developed in 1962. The west face of the existing Rockefeller Center presented an unbroken, cliff-like façade rising from the sidewalk. When the older part of the Center had been built, the El filled Sixth Avenue and there was no way of making the street level attractive. Upon the erection of the new Time & Life Building, however, the Center had stretched physically across the avenue and a visual connection with the original Center was a definite aesthetic requirement. This bonding between old and new would be accomplished between 1962 and 1974 (when the last of the four new Rockefeller Center buildings opened) by means of plazas, which were intended to provide inviting spaces and to recall the traditions of the Center.

The plazas surrounding the Time & Life, Exxon, McGraw-Hill, and Celanese Buildings qualify as urban art themselves and they are embellished—as are the older Rockefeller Center buildings—by commissioned art as well. Whereas the art in the original part of the Center attempted to symbolize humanitarian and philosophical themes, however, the new art tends toward functional amenities and parks and abstract sculptures.

The parks to the west of (in fact, behind) the Exxon and McGraw-Hill Buildings were installed not so much for reasons of aesthetics or tradition but because of the city's building codes, which demand additional street level space to compensate for buildings built above a certain height. The McGraw-Hill minipark with its trees, chairs, and tables is particularly successful, thanks to the playful tunnel which penetrates a dividing wall door, down which cascades an overflowing waterfall. This pleasant feature was inspired perhaps by a similar structure at the World's Fair of 1939 (to which Wallace Harrison, one of the Center's architects, was an important contributor). Thus, again, at the Center practical necessity has become a permanent delight, all within a grand tradition.

The contemporary art in Rockefeller Center glorifies the abstract and kinetic work of recent decades, such as the two-colored sidewalk with its swirl pattern at the Time & Life Building. Top left: a tapestry reproduction of Pablo Picasso's 1924 theater curtain "Mercure" enhances the Exxon Building lobby; bottom left: a mini-park west of the McGraw-Hill Building draws visitors through a "wall of water"; top center: the "Cubed Curve" by William Crovello distinguishes the Americas Plaza in front of the Time & Life Building. In the lobby of the Exxon Building "Moon and Stars" is suspended in gilded bronze from the ceiling, top right. Bottom right: the sides of the "Sun Triangle" point to the four seasonal positions of the sun at solar noon in New York.

When Radio City Music Hall opened its doors on December 27, 1932, it was the grandest, best-equipped theater in America. Millions came to applaud.

CHAPTER THREE
Showplace of the Nation

THE CALM, confident look of Rockefeller Center, the limestone dignity of its older buildings, and the lordly ramparts of its new cross-the-avenue extension all combine to belie the inherently precarious nature of Rockefeller Center's success. The success of the Center is not only hard-won but never entirely secure.

What makes the Center's success precarious is the uniquely dual nature of the place. It is both a commercial venture and a personal memorial to the benevolent spirit who boldly launched the enterprise more than half a century ago. As a commercial venture it must garner profits, often by changing with the times. As a personal memorial it must remain recognizably the same, for a memorial that is drastically altered is a poor monument indeed. To the management of Rockefeller Center, lasting success means striking a balance between profits and permanence. The inner history of Rockefeller Center is the struggle to maintain that precarious balance in the teeth of time, change, and inevitable decay.

In this sense, the history of Radio City Music Hall, the second Center building to open, is the epitome of the entire Rockefeller Center story. Like that larger story it is a history highlighted by grand ambitions, unforeseen events, stunning failure, and, most important, the Center's gritty determination to triumph over adversity.

That there is a Radio City Music Hall at all is due to an accident of corporate history. In 1929 David Sarnoff, the empire-building head of RCA, joined hands with Joseph Kennedy, father of the future president of the United States, to create a seemingly powerful new movie company known as RKO. When RCA signed up as tenant number one in the Rockefeller development, its bumptious fledgling subsidiary put itself down for two theaters and promised the country that it would "develop a standard of entertainment for Radio City which has never been realized in the way of popular amusements."

This was partly ballyhoo, to use the term of the day, but not entirely. Rockefeller felt strongly that if his costly development was to become a home for "popular amusements" they had better be something the likes of which had never been seen before.

No sooner did Rockefeller's entertainment requirements become known to the sharp-witted denizens of the Great White Way, than there appeared on the Rockefeller doorstep the one man in America gifted enough to satisfy them and confident enough to leap at the opportunity.

His real name, Samuel Lionel Rothafel, meant nothing to most Americans, but his nickname was almost as famous as Babe Ruth's. He was the flam-

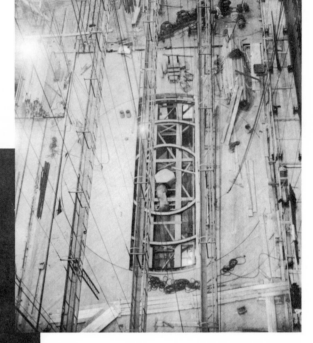

The revolving area (circular outline) is part of the Music Hall's stage—the biggest ever.

Samuel Lionel Rothafel, known as "Roxy," was the flamboyant, glamorous theater entrepreneur who planned the Music Hall.

boyant "Roxy," the extravagant genius who had turned the exhibition of movies into a peculiar hybrid art form unique to America. He was also simple, lovable Roxy, of "Roxy and His Gang," the star of NBC radio and one of the first radio performers to discover that a friendly intimate manner— "Goodnight, Pleasant Dreams, God Bless You" was his famous sign-off—could captivate an unseen audience of millions. He was Roxy, the P.T. Barnum of twentieth-century mass entertainment, the unrivaled master of palatial theater design, spectacular stagecraft, and the psychology of theater audiences.

His originality was striking. It was Roxy, an ex-Marine from Stillwater, Minnesota, who had virtu-

Arches of light surround the theatergoer in the Music Hall.

Radio City Music Hall would provide the only competition to "Roxy's" own theaters.

ally invented the "stage show," an elaborate program of "atmospheric prologues," synchronized orchestral music, and dramatic vignettes, designed to enhance and intensify the experience of movie-going in the days of the silent film. It was Roxy who forged the link between movies and symphonic "soundtrack" music which has never been broken to this day in America, although it never took hold beyond our shores. It was Roxy, too, who introduced courteous ushers, indeed courtesy in general, to movie-going, which had been in pre-Roxy days a pretty rough-and-ready affair. Respect for the ordinary person was perhaps Roxy's most winning trait. It was Roxy, the devoted egalitarian, who insisted that

The lobbies, auditorium, and stage for the Music Hall were intended to be so magnificent that theatergoers would feel as if they were part of the performance—and with rising excitement. Peter Clark, right, designer of the stage, examines a model of the three levels which can be raised 13 feet and lowered 27, a technical marvel.

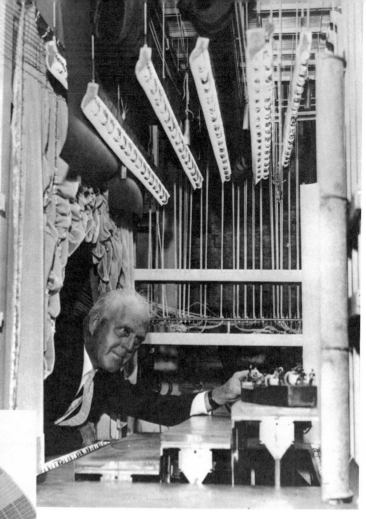

Leon Leonidoff, left, and Russell Markert, right, devised brilliant stage spectaculars.

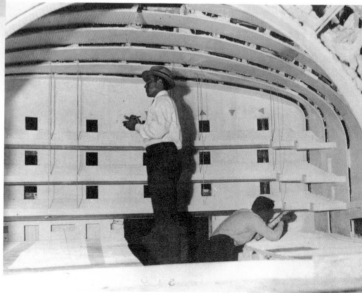

A two-ton plaster model of the Music Hall interior was assembled on the floor of the auditorium.

the general public had better taste than it was given credit for and who introduced into his stage shows condensed ballets, operatic arias, and the more melodic portions of the classic symphonic repertoire. In 1927 Roxy, then forty-five, had reached what seemed like the zenith of his meteoric career when he took charge of the largest and most lavishly equipped theater in the world, just one block due west of Columbia's Upper Estate. Having no false modesty he called it the Roxy, and every smalltown Roxy theater, dance hall, and diner pays tribute to the man, his movie house, and the captivating combination of elegance and equality that they so effectively embodied.

Less famous now, Rothafel in his heyday was a compelling figure who enthralled all who met him, including John D. Rockefeller, Jr., who found himself "impressed," he wrote Todd, by Roxy's "simplicity, his idealism, his fine spirit, and his genius, as well as by his breadth of vision and grasp of practical matters." The Rothafel combination of democracy and sophistication was particularly appealing to Rockefeller. With the latter's approval RKO acquired Roxy's costly services "in connection with the theaters to be operated by RKO in the new Radio City-Rockefeller development," as RKO's publicity office proudly announced on April 9, 1931.

What Roxy had in mind for the "Radio City-Rockefeller development" gladdened the hearts of all concerned with it. For one thing, Roxy (who was

The sumptuous lobby spaces were designed in high Art Deco, giving visitors an exciting welcome.

Donald Deskey's Music Hall interiors were witty Art Deco combinations of sleek geometric forms and comfortable organic surfaces.

tending toward megalomania) hoped to create in Radio City a theater that was even bigger, better, and more awe-inspiring than his own Roxy Theater. That is to say, he planned to surpass his only serious rival, namely, himself. Secondly, he wanted his new theater to show no movies at all. It would be a "music hall," wherein Roxy, the master of the stage show, would revive a more modern and dynamic version of vaudeville, whose popular return to favor he firmly believed was at hand.

Although that belief would swiftly prove to be absolutely false—the mistake would bring about Roxy's ruin—Rothafel's reasoning was based on a truth that would one day catch up with Radio City Music Hall. Rothafel believed that the movie-plus-stage-show format that he had invented was doomed by the coming of sound. Talkies, he insisted, could stand on their own two feet. They did not require, as the silents did, the elaborate support of live entertainment. Since the movie-plus-stage-show was widely believed to have "killed" vaudeville, the talk-

ing picture *minus* stage show, reasoned Roxy, would help re-create a demand for it. Of course it could not come back unaltered. Roxy understood this quite well. It would have to be super-vaudeville in a super-music hall. From Rockefeller on down, everybody believed that this was just what the Rockefeller development needed in its new "entertainment center" phase. That Roxy might be completely misreading the public mood never entered anyone's mind. He had followed his intuition about public taste for two decades and had never once been wrong.

Somewhat illogically, however, the old Roxy format of film and stage show, presumably doomed, was to be carried on in the second of the two RKO theaters, one block south on Sixth Avenue. This "New Roxy Theater," as it was to be called, was a mere 3,500-seat baby compared to the 6,000 seat Music Hall which Roxy, in concert with the Associated Architects, a bevy of technical experts, and a special design team began to plan and build in the

The second mezzanine ladies' lounge, designed by Deskey, placed chrome and leather against a mural by Yasuo Kuniyoshi.

*The first mezzanine ladies' lounge
multiplied the illusions of beauty
with angled mirrors.*

summer of 1931. Progress was swift. In June 1932 the Music Hall was nearly complete, and a leading exponent of the new "Art Deco" design style named Donald Deskey was awarded the coveted contract to carry out a completely unified scheme of interior decoration for the theater. In November 1932 Rockefeller paid the Music Hall a visit and came away more thoroughly delighted with the place than he would be with any other single building in Rockefeller Center. "The great auditorium is beautiful, soul-satisfying, inspiring beyond anything I have dreamed possible." The Grand Foyer, he said, "is as distinguished and unusual and truly impressive as the theater itself," especially "the great simplicity of the wall spaces with their long brilliant mirrors." As for the various lounges and smoking rooms designed by the brilliant Deskey, they, too,

delighted Rockefeller, who had hired Deskey to do some interior design work for his own house a few years before. "These rooms are all of them, interesting, unusual and distinguished to an extraordinary degree. There is a style and a chic about the whole building which is impressive in the extreme."

Rockefeller's taste was excellent. The Music Hall is both an acknowledged masterpiece of theater design and a major achievement in Art Deco "style and chic."

As far as theater design was concerned, what the architects and designers had done was give form to certain guiding principles laid down by Roxy. Among other things, the master showman wanted the Music Hall to induce in its customers a heightened sense of tingling anticipation with every step toward their seats that they took. This was one aspect of Roxy's general theory that the theater was a vital part of the show, a theory whose validity the history of the Music Hall was to demonstrate. To achieve this heightened expectation the designers directed the ticketholders through three dramatically contrasted spaces. The first was the ticket lobby, with its low black ceiling, the squat antithesis of the next step. This was the Grand Foyer, which was not only long and narrow but had a ceiling 60 feet high. The designers underscored its dramatic height and narrowness with two slender 29-foot-long chandeliers and with the towering wall mirrors that Rockefeller had so admired. High, narrow, and brightly lit, the palatial foyer stands in contrast both to the lobby and to perhaps the most breathtaking auditorium ever created.

Following Roxy's instructions, the architects, led by the versatile Wallace Harrison, had created an immense darkened space uncluttered by looming balconies, the latter a point of great importance to Roxy, who thought overhanging balconies split the audience in half. It is a space enveloped by a "ceiling" that curves continuously down to the floor in a sweeping 180-degree arc. It is space that seems to pulsate and throb, the feeling of life and motion intensified by the ceiling's unique design: eight enormous arching bands that seem to radiate from the stage like waves from a giant source of light.

The modernity of the auditorium was fittingly enhanced by Deskey's interior design. He had vowed to make the Music Hall's interior "completely and uncompromisingly modern in effect" and he had succeeded splendidly. By "contemporary" Deskey meant Art Deco (short for the French "art decoratif"), a style which had as its primary inspiration the clean, curving lines and gleaming surfaces of modern machinery and modern, machine-made products. Machine-age design and the use of industrial materials were characteristic Art Deco hallmarks. For the Music Hall, Deskey, another child of smalltown Minnesota, commissioned aluminum statues, designed gun-metal mirrors and lighting fixtures fashioned of steel, chrome, and bakelite. He papered walls with aluminum foil and a new synthetic called permatex. In the hands of Deskey, Art Deco became more than novel materials and sleek machine-tooled geometry, for he played games with the geometry itself, as if mocking the machine-age style's limitations. For thin, tubular chair legs, he designed fat, bulging leather seats. Against gleam-

Every detail, including signs, was designed with style.

Wall lighting fixtures, designed by Deskey and the architects.

The architects' attention to detail is seen in this brass railing panel with its lyre design.

ing chrome and polished steel he placed pigskin and pony hide, suede and white kid, a contrast of the metallic and the organic that has helped give Deskey's Music Hall interiors an enduring power to charm. "Visual jazz," as one art critic has called them.

Opposite: one of Roxy's dicta was that ordinary people deserved courtesy. The ushers provided that.

The enormous and elaborate "Mighty Wurlitzer" organ provided music.

The world-famed Rockettes first lined up in 1932.

The Rockettes were first known as the "Rockets" and then as the "Roxyettes." Here they compete with the Corps de Ballet to advertise "The Adventures of Robin Hood."

If the architects and designers had given Roxy the modern theater he wanted, the engineers gave him the stage he demanded. It was—and still is—the largest and best-equipped stage in the world. Its three lengthwise sections can each be raised 13 feet above stage level and lowered 27 feet below it by huge lifts of such advanced design that the Department of War was to make use of the system during World War II and treat it as a military secret. The stage contained, in addition, a revolving circular section that is 43 feet in diameter. The seventy-five-piece orchestra, carried in a special band car, can go above the stage, below the stage, across the stage and under the stage. It can disappear from out front and re-emerge at stage rear. The stage has equipment that can send up towering fountains of water or bring down cascades of rain. The light console, far in advance of its time, can turn the great auditorium into an extension of the stage and the audience into part of the spectacle, another Roxy principle. The great stage curtain, driven by thirteen motors, can produce so many patterned shapes that Roxy decided to make it the first act of his opening show.

Thus, with the help of the most spectacular of auditoriums, the most modern of theater interiors, and the most advanced of stage equipment, vaudeville would have its "renaissance" at the Radio City Music Hall, or so Roxy confidently promised the readers of *Woman's Home Companion*.

The great Music Hall opening, long and eagerly anticipated by the press (which found the unlikely combination of Rockefeller and Roxy irresistible), fell on the evening of December 27, 1932. Some 6,000 people lucky enough or influential enough to obtain tickets thronged into the lobby under a torrent of ice-cold rain. As one ticketholder recalled thirty years later, it was "one of the final gloomy

The Rockettes, pretending here to be a watchband in a 1939 performance of "The Clocks," united the old vaudeville days with modern cinema.

The Corps de Ballet of the Music Hall illustrated "Roxy" Rothafel's belief that everyday folk appreciated quality performance.

The unsparing splendor of the Rockettes' costumes helped bring them success and respect.

89

days of an exceedingly gloomy year." In attendance were magnates of industry—Walter Chrysler, for one; lords of the press—William Randolph Hearst most conspicuously; giants of show business—Charlie Chaplin, Clark Gable, Noel Coward, Irving Berlin. And, of course, the Rockefeller family.

As the huge audience filed toward its red plush seats for the 8:15 curtain, scarcely anyone could have known that if he wished to see the entire show

Russell Markert, kneeling, was the founder of the Radio City Music Hall Rockettes dance troupe, and trained generations of Rockettes with calisthentics.

Sparkling precision marked the Rockettes' twice-daily show.

he would have to stay seated until 2:30 in the morning. Act followed polished act in a seemingly interminable procession: choral singing and solo singing, six kinds of dance numbers, skits, blackouts, dramatic vignettes, and comic routines, an incredible twenty acts in all. It was as if Roxy, fearing deep down that something was amiss, hoped to disguise it by sheer abundance. There were numerous fine moments, of course. The Wallendas did their great aerial act on the circus-sized stage. Ray Bolger, the "outstanding young American dancing comedian," disported there too, after the Tuskegee Institute's famed chorus sang "Trampin." The Rockettes, already famous, made their Music Hall debut as the "Roxyettes."

It was both too much and not enough. By the time Martha Graham and her modern dance troupe performed their "Choric Dance for an Antique Greek Tragedy"—act eighteen—half the theater was empty and the critics had long since departed to pound out next morning's reviews. Those were hostile at worst and puzzled at best. How could Roxy, the master showman, expect to revive "variety" in a theater so much larger than vaudeville audiences were accustomed to? Was the public really hungry for super-vaudeville?

The answer to that was simple: No. The "music hall" show at the Music Hall was an instant and total flop; within two weeks it had lost an appalling $180,000. In desperation RKO switched to the

All Rockettes productions were conceived, choreographed, and costumed at Radio City Music Hall.

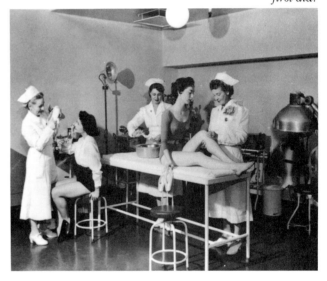

Rockettes received regular care with health checkups and first aid.

established movie-plus-stage-show format (thereby condemning the New Roxy Theater down the block to a long twilight existence until the wrecker's ball demolished it in 1954). Stunned and disgraced by his failure, Roxy, in mid-January, left for an extended southern vacation, a broken man who had been physically ailing for some time, with but three more years to live.

Two weeks after that RKO, too, left the scene as it slid bankrupt into the hands of receivers. Rockefeller Center in due course would take over management of the Music Hall. By a totally unpredictable concatenation of events, the officers of Rockefeller Center Inc. had been pushed, willy-nilly, into show business, about which they knew little except that stage shows were expensive, that the mammoth theater was hard to fill, and that despite the change of format, the Music Hall was still losing money. As one Music Hall old-timer said: "all we had then were a lot of expenses and very little income."

Once more greeted by jeers and mockery, Rockefeller and his managerial team did not lose heart. Neither did they lose their heads. One thing they clearly grasped. Despite Roxy's colossal blunder he had left Rockefeller Center a priceless legacy: a masterpiece of theater design and gifted backstage personnel. Under the leadership of Russell Markert, the Rockettes were destined to become the leading precision-line dancers in the world; in 1937 they would take first prize at the Paris Exposition. Under the superb choreography of Florence Rogge, Roxy's Music Hall Corps de Ballet would offer skilled condensations of ballet classics—*Swan Lake*, *Coppelia*—to a public more fond of ballet than they themselves had imagined. In the hands of Leon Leonidoff, director of production, the Music Hall had a showman marvelously skilled at extracting every conceivable advantage from the theater's lavish stage equipment.

Given such assets the Center management was convinced that the Music Hall would one day catch on with the public. Until it did, Rockefeller Center

Between the opening of the Music Hall in the 1930s and its waning popularity in the 1970s, a total of 250 million people flocked in, like these waiting for tickets.

Inc. was determined to keep up every appearance of success. Fighting on every front in the difficult days of 1933, Rockefeller Center simply could not afford even the suspicion of failure in its first and most publicized building. Despite the continuing losses at the box office, the Center management would brook no skimping on the Music Hall's costly stage shows. To ensure a well-filled house, as one of the Music Hall's first managers recalled, the box office was given the power to accept, in lieu of cash, I.O.U.'s and post-dated checks from the customers. "Anything to get the people in."

It was an arduous, uphill struggle, but Roxy's crystal ball had only been half-clouded. The stage show format *was* something of an anachronism in the era of talking pictures. By the mid-1930s a number of movie "palaces" were beginning to abandon live entertainment. In conspicuous contrast, the mid-1930s marked the first profitable years for the Music Hall, which, like the larger Center, was bucking the trend of the times. Just as the Center managers had expected, the great theater and the peerless stage shows were inexorably exerting their powers of attraction. Although palatial movie theaters were common enough in the 1930s, if you had not seen the Music Hall's auditorium there was absolutely nothing in your prior experience to prepare you for the cascading splendor of that immense curving space. Chorus lines, too, were hardy show business perennials, but the Rockettes captivated an entire country. When they finished one of their astonishing dance drills with a front-of-the-stage high kick in unison, they were greeted with thunderous applause, twice a day, day after day, year after year.

Nor was that all there was to the Music Hall's suc-cess. With the shrewdness of veteran impresarios (although they were in show business but a matter of months) Rockefeller Center's management linked the Music Hall to the most universally celebrated occasions—the Christmas and Easter holidays. The Music Hall's Christmas Spectacular, inaugurated in 1933 and repeated annually, was meant to become a recognized institution and to an amazing degree it became just that. Every Christmas season it drew people in such numbers that it generated perhaps the longest lines that ever snaked and re-snaked around a movie theater.

By the 1940s Radio City Music Hall had become the biggest single attraction in New York City—a "must" for visitors to the city as well as the ultimate holiday treat for millions of New Yorkers as well. It was also one of Hollywood's most glittering prizes.

Rockefeller Center has always nurtured a versatile public image. Here poodles show obedience instruction at National Dog Week.

The skating rink opened in 1936, making the sunken plaza an outdoor stage on which anybody with a pair of skates could twirl about. Millions have done so.

Celebration of holidays has given the Center a community role. The bunny garden was an Easter feature in 1936.

Easter at the Center

The annual Easter concert of 1943 was beamed over short wave radio to United States troops in Europe and the Orient. The choristers were business people who worked in Rockefeller Center.

Several hundred Easter lilies adorn the Channel Gardens during Easter Week.

The Easter Parade of Sunday strollers surges around plantings of lilies and tulips in 1961.

In 1936, three-year-old Bruce Martin was dressed up in a bunny suit and allowed to play with the prize bunnies in the plaza.

The Center Theater, which opened in 1932 seating 3,500 people, was demolished in 1954; the Music Hall had captured its audience with the decision to show movies.

To have one's film chosen for a Radio City Music Hall premiere was a prized achievement for a film producer. It put the stamp of sterling worth on the few that were chosen of the many that were screened. To have one's film chosen for the Christmas season was true glory indeed and not a little gold as well. After an exclusive first run at the Music Hall, a well-received Christmas-time movie would be welcomed by a public panting to see it. Such was the prestige of "The Showplace of the Nation," as the Music Hall came to be known.

Pushed into the waters of show business, Rockefeller Center's management quickly developed a marked aptitude for putting on shows outside as well as inside the Music Hall. The lower plaza, the

Promenade, and the private street formed superb outdoor stages and the Center quickly made the most of them. The management's most memorable production made its debut in early December 1933—the first formal and ceremonious lighting of the Center's towering, bedazzling Christmas trees, a seemingly local affair that has become yet another Center-created institution, one that is enjoyed by many millions each year over television. In May 1934 the Center staged the first of hundreds of special events in the lower plaza when it treated passersby to a concert by the famed John Philip Sousa band. Over the years, the plaza area has been the scene of so many civic rallies, dignitary-welcomings, and fund-raising drives (not to mention fashion shows, amateur boxing, and ice-sculpting competitions) that it has taken on the aspect of a metropolitan village green. During World War II,

Eugene Schoen was responsible for the interior decoration of the Center Theater. Less showy than Deskey's at Radio City, it was distinguished by a Steichen photo-mural in the men's lounge.

Typical of the more restrained interiors of the Center Theater was this glass mural showing Amelia Earhart crossing the Atlantic. Sixteen feet long, the mural was paint fused by heat on glass.

Rockefeller Center's "This Is Our War" exhibitions—"Know Your Enemy" was one—made the plaza and Promenade look for months like the cockpit of the domestic war effort.

After the expansion across the Avenue of the Americas, the managerial showmen of Rockefeller Center, veterans by now, found themselves with five handsome new "stages" to fill. They cheerfully did so by staging folk concerts, dance exhibitions, craft demonstrations (including sheep-shearing), and innumerable other small-scale productions in the plazas fronting the new buildings and in the "mini-park" behind the Exxon Building. The Center's growth has given an enormous boost to outdoor showmanship at Rockefeller Center, but time and change, alas, were not so kind to the Center's first and primary stage, the Music Hall itself.

As late as 1963 the theater's future seemed utterly cloudless. When a *New Yorker* writer decided to mark the passing of its third decade, he took cheerful note of the Music Hall's seemingly unshakeable foundations. It was regularly drawing some six million customers annually, twice as many, the *New Yorker* noted, as the United Nations, the Empire State Building, and the Statue of Liberty combined. That the Music Hall's original rival, the old Roxy Theater, had been demolished in 1960, that every passing year left fewer and fewer movie palaces intact, that the Music Hall, the biggest and best of them all, was now the *only* movie theater in creation that still offered a stage show, were not looked upon as potential danger signs. Such singularity seemed to be unimpeachable proof that the Music Hall existed on a special plateau of its own, immune

OUR ANSWER

UNCONDITIONAL SURRENDER

During World War II Rockefeller
Center mounted displays to
highlight the military campaigns.
"Unconditional Surrender" was
part of the "Nature of the Enemy" show.

"The Four Freedoms" showed the
symbolic figures of Want and Fear
vanquished and Speech and Wor-
ship defended.

98

MILITARIZATION OF CHILDREN

"The passion of the (Samurai) spirit is conveyed in the following stirring words... Even after you have been beheaded in action, your bodiless head should kill one enemy by fastening itself on him by means of the teeth."

CAPTAIN HIDEO HIRAIDE, *March 8, 1942*

FREEDOM·FROM·WANT   FREEDOM·OF·SPEECH

"This Is Our War"

The Center's determination to be engaged with the community around it and the nation and world at large precipitated a series of war tableaux during World War II. The largest bomb ever made in America was displayed, below, while militarization of children was dramatized, above. President Roosevelt's "Four Freedoms" were realized in sculpture, and refugees from Germany spoke.

SLAVE LABOR

to time, change, and decay. It is not "just a place of entertainment," the *New Yorker* writer observed, "it's a national object of pride, like the Grand Canyon," and presumably just as enduringly attractive.

It was in 1968, one of the stormiest years in American political history, that the danger signs first began to be recognized. By 1971, *Newsweek* was reporting somberly on what it called, revealingly, "Trouble in Paradise." The seemingly impregnable Music Hall, said the magazine, "is besieged by the twin torments of changing values and escalating costs." By then it seemed as if every aspect of the turbulent 1970s was laying siege to the Music Hall. Revolt in the ghettos struck terror in the hearts of suburbanites; fewer and fewer came to visit a city they believed to be haunted by crime. The increasing independence of children barely out of their teens was eroding the central element in the Music Hall's popular support, the close-knit family for whom the Music Hall's entertainment fare had been especially designed. The "changing values" noted in passing by *Newsweek* pervaded every aspect of American society, altering the repute of everything. Established heroes were suspect, established institutions lost their luster. What parents admired their children scorned. In the general challenge to well-established powers, the Music Hall's prestige faded inexorably. Film producers refused to grant it exclu-

A dramatic and narrative addition to Rockefeller Center's entertainment program in the 1970s was "The New York Experience."

"The New York Experience" was advertised as "surrounding the audience with sights, sounds, and multi-sensory special effects."

100

sive first-run rights, for its seal of approval meant little to millions of teenagers who now formed the bulk of the movie-going audience. The "Showplace of the Nation" ceased to be a "must" for visitors to New York. Under Hollywood's new rating system, many of the movies that drew big crowds were simply unsuitable for a theater famed for its family-oriented Christmas and Easter shows.

Up against social change in its most acute form, the managers of Rockefeller Center were keenly

Rockefeller Center. This time it did not. Between 1967 and 1977 the Music Hall's audiences dwindled from an average of five million a year to less than two million—and box office losses mounted correspondingly. The singularity of Radio City Music Hall, once the hallmark of its special grace, now seemed the measure of its hopelessly outdated character.

On January 5, 1978, after desperately trying to negotiate a life-saving contract with a major Holly-

The lower plaza remained a dependable tourist attraction, winter and summer, despite changing times and tastes.

The Rainbow Room at the top of the RCA Building is an eternally fashionable night spot overlooking the lights of the city below.

aware that their license to change accordingly was limited. As Alton G. Marshall, then-president of Rockefeller Center, Inc., reminded a *Newsweek* reporter: "We present entertainment of quality, good taste and high moral values. Our audience expects family entertainment and we have to keep faith with them."

Year after year, that audience continued to shrink: fewer touring families, fewer suburbanites in for the day, and a growing scarcity of tasteful Hollywood films to choose from. In the past, persistence in adversity had often succeeded at

In the mid-1960s half a million visitors a year were enjoying the view from the RCA Building Observation Roof.

wood studio, Alton Marshall called a press conference in the Rockettes' small rehearsal hall. What he had to say left his listeners stunned and angry. "I am announcing the closing of Radio City Music Hall at the end of the 1978 Easter season on April 12, because we can no longer sustain the losses which reached $2.3 million in 1977 and are projected at $3.5 million for 1978." The failed Hollywood negotiations, explained Marshall, had proven the final straw. As to the physical fate of the Music Hall, that was up in the air, but Marshall left little doubt that it was in for a drastic overhaul if not treatment more drastic yet. The Center's quest for permanence had wiped out profits for years. Now its continuing financial losses seemed about to alter forever a major element of Rockefeller Center; management was apparently ready to drop the cur-

tain on the grandest and brightest stage in the world.

That was not to be, however. Nobody has ever surpassed the management of Rockefeller Center at the art of turning commercial ventures and promotional gambits into beloved institutions. Just how brilliantly those popular policies had succeeded in regard to the Music Hall swiftly became apparent in the aftermath of the press conference. Some 250 million paying customers— a truly staggering figure—had been entertained at Radio City Music Hall since its grand opening in 1928. They had come

A children's hockey team, opposite, looks south from the RCA Building Observation Roof.

away with happy memories, often enough the most powerfully nostalgic of memories: the recollection of childhood at Christmas time. For countless millions of Americans the prospect of the Radio City Music Hall ceasing to exist was literally unbearable. Popular opposition to change at the Music Hall quickly became a force to be reckoned with, espe-cially when state and city officials joined the chorus of opposition. Moreover, the Music Hall was not only a cherished memory and a municipal asset; by now it had entered the annals of American art and design. Heads of important museums, leading architects, theater people, esteemed conservation organizations, officials of the Smithsonian Institution, citi-

Rockefeller Center has always had official visitors like the small state-within-a-state that it is. Ghana's President Dr. Nkrumah, center, visited in the 1960s.

Princess Margaret of Great Britain and her husband, Lord Snowden, right, are escorted along Rockefeller Plaza during an official visit to the Center.

Don Elliott plays during "Music for a City Evening" in the Exxon Park.

Spanish flamenco dancers click castanets during a noontime concert.

A daytime concert in the Center features Odetta, the popular folk singer.

zens in all walks of life, began calling on the New York Landmarks Preservation Commission to designate Radio City Music Hall—from its great auditorium to its telephone alcove, from its Grand Foyer to the very grilles covering the firehoses—an official Interior Landmark, and hence legally unalterable. On March 28, 1978 the Commission did just that.

The public had secured the Music Hall's permanence. It was up to Rockefeller Center, however, to make it profitable once more, a truly herculean task. One thing the management knew all too well after years of wrestling with the problem: the old movie-plus-stage-show format had to be abandoned. Every social change undergone by America had conspired to kill it at last. On April 25, 1979 the final curtain fell on the last performance in that forty-seven-year-old Music Hall tradition. Within days, Rockefeller Center's newly created entertainment arm, Radio City Music Hall Productions, got started on a swift and costly program of restoring the entire Music Hall interior, down to the smallest landmarked detail, to the sparkling mint condition of 1932. Well before that, the management had drawn up the basic plan for the Music Hall's economic recovery. Movies would no longer be shown on a regular basis. The centerpiece of entertainment would henceforth be full-length contemporary stage presentations, with the Rockettes, abiding stars, forming the main bridge to the

glorious past. Thus, by a full turn of fortune's wheel, Roxy's original movie-less live entertainment had returned to Rockefeller Center.

The new stage presentations—ten new shows a year—form only a fraction, however, of the revived Music Hall's activities. Just as Rockefeller Center's rental office had used every asset it could muster in its desperate Depression hunt for tenants, so its entertainment arm had been trying to wring every advantage from the assets of the Music Hall. In order to make the fullest possible use of the great auditorium, Radio City Music Hall Productions has been able to turn the theater into one of the premier popular concert halls in the country. From Pavarotti to Diana Ross, from Frank Sinatra to Linda Ronstadt, some fifty major concerts a year are now produced at the Music Hall. The vast auditorium, never easy to fill, is now the scene, too, of enormous industrial shows and famed award-giving ceremonies. Nor has the "style and chic" of the Music Hall's public rooms been neglected. They now provide the setting for gala corporate celebrations and receptions.

The reinvigorated activities of the Music Hall are not confined to the theater itself. They have spread across the country. The Music Hall's managers now send Music Hall shows on tour and even produce shows that will never play at the Music Hall. Experienced in large-scale productions, they have put on concerts in such awesomely difficult places as the Superdome in New Orleans. Drawing on that same unique experience, the production company has served as consultant to the Knoxville World's Fair as well as to shopping centers and exhibition halls across the country. In its struggle for economic recovery, Rockefeller Center's management has turned the Music Hall into a national entertainment enterprise. It is change in the service of permanence, the exact epitome of the larger Center.

In a tone of mingled envy and awe, a New York realtor once spoke of what he called "Rockefeller Center's passionate predilection for remaining young." He was thinking, in part, of the expansion across the Avenue of the Americas, which created a crisply contemporary companion to John D. Rockefeller, Jr.'s original development. He was thinking, too, of the perennial sparkle of the "old" Center, where the well-cleaned limestone walls look as fresh and as noble as ever, where fifty-year-old machinery works with the reliability of the very latest equipment, where brass rails and fittings still gleam brightly, and where the Concourse shops have become, if anything, more brightly attractive than ever. Youthfulness, however, is not really the Center's true nature, for there are features of Rockefeller Center which have a wonderfully old-fashioned quality about them—to mention two, the Easter "fashion show" in the Promenade and the courteous, uniformed personnel (who look as if they had stepped straight out of the 1930s). The real and abiding passion of Rockefeller Center is its determination to preserve its distinction, its personality, and its hard-won place in the American firmament.

Such is the story of Rockefeller Center. Remember, it is a story that began when some discontented operagoers decided it was time to move grand opera "uptown," thereby setting in motion a chain of events and actions with a most unlikely result. Citizens of varying ambitions and motivations and talents struggled with or against each other to produce a compromise for their time. By that act, something else happened: the timeless creation of a world-famous piece of real estate, an architectural masterpiece, and a national institution.

On June 16, 1982, an 8-foot tall, 1,200-pound cake in the form of key Center buildings was cut by Richard A. Voell, president and chief-executive-officer, and David Rockefeller, chairman of Rockefeller Center, both at left, and Joseph Barkan, president of the NYC board of education, representing the students who baked the Center's 50th anniversary cake.

Portfolio: Christmas in the Center

Traditions are implicit statements of faith, made by people who thus reaffirm their goodwill toward each other. For five decades Christmas in Rockefeller Center has been a tradition.

Since 1931 when workmen gathered around a tree they had decorated themselves, a tree which thrust its branches toward the sky from a muddy construction site, Christmas in Rockefeller Center has been the luminous culmination of each year. In 1933 the first formally trimmed tree was erected in front of the 70-story RCA Building, which had just been completed that May. The tree was trimmed with 700 blue and white lights; two church choirs and the Columbia University Glee Club heralded its lighting. Over the years the trees—usually Norway or white spruce—have come from New York, New Jersey, New England, and, occasionally, more distant places. In 1966 the first tree from outside the United States was presented by Canada in honor of the Centennial of its Confederation. Since 1971 the trees, which have ranged from 50 to 70 feet high and weighed as much as ten tons, have been recycled after they were taken down, with environmental concerns in mind. The average tree has provided as much as three tons of ground cover for horticultural use.

In the fifty Christmases since 1933 the season has been marked not only by the trees, but also by choristers, ice-skating pageants, home-town carolers, and special decorations in the Channel Gardens and the Promenade. In 1950, for instance, a ceiling of electric stars in which the major constellations glowed was suspended over the Promenade.

Since 1958 English-born sculptor Valerie Clarebout has fashioned displays from brass and aluminum wire for the Channel Gardens. The first year the opening words of C.F. Alexander's hymn of 1848, "All things bright and beautiful, all creatures great and small. . ." inspired sculptures of deer, rabbits, squirrels, chipmunks, birds, and even a skunk. Since 1970 Miss Clarebout's twelve wire-sculpted angels have trumpeted the joys of the season.

At the Center, Christmas is truly "all things bright and beautiful."

The Rockettes, the greatest precision dancers in the world, salute as tin soldiers in the Christmas Pageant.

Christmas trees, sprinkled with starry lights, are reflected in the pool of the Time & Life Building.

Gossamer angels lift golden trumpets down the Promenade of the Channel Gardens to herald the Christmas season.

Gigantic snowmen seem to playfully hurry away from the towering Rockefeller Center Christmas tree in 1961.

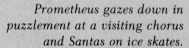

Prometheus gazes down in puzzlement at a visiting chorus and Santas on ice skates.

While tree lights twinkle, a band of tubas blares in the happy tumult of the season.

From the time the first one rose in 1933, the Rockefeller Center Christmas tree has been the nation's symbol for festivity and merriment. The skating rink transforms the plaza into winter holiday guise.

THE GUIDE

Rockefeller Center, the world's largest privately owned business and entertainment center, fills nearly twenty-two acres in the heart of New York City with skyscrapers, roof gardens, a theater, a Promenade, and even a winter skating rink and a private street. Known as the "city-within-a-city," Rockefeller Center provides its tenants with office space, some thirty-five restaurants, and an indoor subway station shopping Concourse. Residents and visitors to New York frequent more than two hundred shops, drug stores, doctors, dentists, and banks. The Center is connected to the United States government by a Post Office, a Passport Agency, and an office of the National Weather Service. International relations are furthered by the presence of fourteen foreign consulates and some ninety travel offices.

More than any urban complex, Rockefeller Center *is* complex. With seventy stories above ground and six levels below, with miles of underground concourse, the Center must be mapped to be understood. The following six pages set forth maps and a three-level Directory to facilitate the movements of visitors and tenants, shoppers and undercover passageway seekers. It has been said of Rockefeller Center, that you can do almost anything there. In the following pages you can find out how.

The Center's history is replete with overlapping events and startling "firsts." To present that story in the most concise form, a Chronology has been prepared (pages 120 and 121) based on the lengthier narration which accompanies Rockefeller Center's fiftieth anniversary exhibit (on view in the Center's lower Concourse).

As a further guide to an understanding of the Center's creation, on pages 122 and 123 you can read the statements of purpose and commitments made by the architects, summations by public figures who have performed and visited here, and the words of John D. Rockefeller, Jr., himself. Finally, in the pages just before the Index, we leave you with a round-up of nostalgic postcards which recapitulate the glamour of the Center and of Radio City Music Hall.

Yet the best way to understand the Center is to look at it now with your own perceptions. To have introduced you to that exploration has been the proud purpose of this book.

The angels and their trumpets in the Channel Gardens are only the latest of decades of Christmas Pageant decorations, but from the beginning the ebullience of the season has been celebrated.

Building Directory

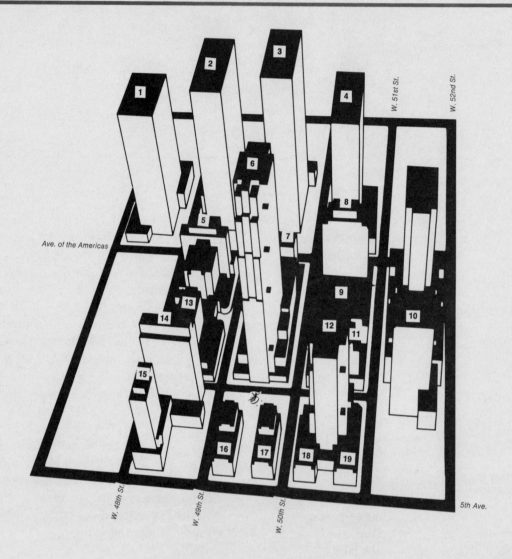

The directory on these two pages refers to shops and services located at mezzanine level or above in each building of Rockefeller Center, as shown on the map. On the following pages are maps and directories of shops and services located at either street or concourse level. Addresses, phone numbers, and map locations are provided for each listing.

11 The Associated Press Building
50 Rockefeller Plz.

17 British Empire Building
620 Fifth Avenue

1 Celanese Building
1211 Ave. of Americas

3 Exxon Building
1251 Ave. of Americas

12 International Building
630 Fifth Ave.

19 International Building North
636 Fifth Ave.

16 La Maison Francaise
610 Fifth Ave.

15 Manufacturers Hanover Trust Building
600 Fifth Ave.

2 McGraw-Hill Building
1221 Ave. of Americas

14 One Rockefeller Plaza Building
One Rockefeller Plaza

18 Palazzo d'Italia
626 Fifth Avenue

9 Radio City Music Hall Entertainment Center
1260 Ave. of Americas

6 RCA Building
30 Rockefeller Plz.

7 RCA Building West
1250 Ave. of Americas

5 Simon & Schuster Building
1230 Ave. of Americas

13 Ten Rockefeller Plaza Building
10 Rockefeller Plz.

4 Time & Life Building
1271 Ave. of Americas

8 1270 Avenue of the Americas Building
1270 Ave. of Americas

10 Warner Communications Building
75 Rockefeller Plz.

Entertainment

6 Rockefeller Center Observation Roof
69th Fl., 30 Rockefeller Plz.
489-2945

Restaurants

6 Rainbow Room/Rainbow Grill
65th Fl., 30 Rockefeller Plz.
757-9090

114

Banks

12 Argentine Banking Corp.
Rm. 514, 630 Fifth Ave. 974-0500

12 Banque Bruxelles Lambert
Rm. 2870, 630 Fifth Ave. 765-8285

8 Banque de L'Indochine et de Suez
10th Fl., 1270 Ave. of Americas
397-9400

12 Deutsche Genossenschaftsbank
Rm. 3350, 630 Fifth Ave. 246-6000

**12 First Interstate International of
California**
33rd Fl., 630 Fifth Ave. 621-0500

15 Nordic American Banking Corp.
16th Fl., 600 Fifth Ave. 765-4800

6 Saudi European Bank, S.A.
Rm. 4525, 30 Rockefeller Plz. 975-0808

12 UMB Bank & Trust Co.
27th Fl., 630 Fifth Ave. 541-8070

Shops & Services

12 Ad-Ex Translation International
Rm. 3004, 630 Fifth Ave. 581-2380

14 Allied Messenger Service, Inc.
Rm. 307, One Rockefeller Plz. 757-8065

**16 Bache Halsey Stuart Shields, Inc.,
brokerage**
Rm. 216, 610 Fifth Ave. 586-7040

**2 Blyth Eastman Paine Webber,
brokerage**
1221 Ave. of Americas 730-8500

8 W.T. Cabe & Co., Inc., brokerage
Rm. 600, 1270 Ave. of Americas
541-6690

12 Cleveland Hair Transplants
Rm. 559, 630 Fifth Ave. 765-7090

11 Commack Coffee Service
50 Rockefeller Plz. 246-4949

**12 Deak-Perera Fifth Ave., Inc.—
Numismatic Div.**
Mezz. 258, 630 Fifth Ave. 757-0100

4 Empire Messenger Service
1271 Ave. of Americas 765-7731

6 Fahnestock & Co., brokerage
Mezz. 25, 30 Rockefeller Plz. 247-8200

**1 Fox Morris Assoc., executive
employment agency**
1211 Ave. of Americas 840-6930

8 Kelly Services, employment agency
1270 Ave. of Americas 489-6137

14 Lazard Freres & Co., brokerage
30th Fl., One Rockefeller Plz. 489-6600

6 Lost & Found, Rockefeller Center
Rm. 240, 30 Rockefeller Plz. 489-2910

**6 Manfra, Tordella & Brookes, Inc.,
numismatists**
30 Rockefeller Plz. 974-3400

2 Merrill Lynch, brokerage
5th Fl., 1221 Ave. of Americas 997-0500

11 Messengers Unlimited
50 Rockefeller Plz. 757-6972

16 Morgans Waterfall & Co., brokerage
Rm. 706, 610 Fifth Ave. 765-3700

**4 Nicholas L. Pliakis, graphics/
photography**
Rm.3741, 1271 Ave. of Americas 582-1861

12 Passport Agency, Department of State
Mezz. 270, 630 Fifth Ave. 541-7700

4 Riom Corp., messenger service
1271 Ave. of Americas 265-5585

3 Shearson Loeb Rhoades, brokerage
11th Fl., 1251 Ave. of Americas 765-7800

**12 Thomson & McKinnon Securities, Inc.,
brokerage**
Rm. 633, 630 Fifth Ave. 582-5011

14 Valley Forge Flag Co., Inc., flags
Rm. 1502, One Rockefeller Plz. 586-1776

6 Vogler Carpets
Mezz. 16, 30 Rockefeller Plz. 765-8600

4 Wagner Photoprint Co., Inc.
Basement Mezz. 16,
1271 Ave. of Americas 245-4796

Travel Information

16 Antigua, Gov't. of
Rm. 311, 610 Fifth Ave. 541-4117

14 Arista World Travel, Inc.
Rm. 1010, One Rockefeller Plz. 541-9190

8 Aruba Concorde-Hotel & Casino Inc.
Rm. 2304, 1270 Ave. of Americas
757-8989

8 Aruba Tourist Bureau
Rm. 2212, 1270 Ave. of Americas
246-3030

12 Australian Consulate
4th Fl., 630 Fifth Ave. 245-4000

12 Australian Information Service
4th Fl., 630 Fifth Ave. 245-4000

12 Australian Tourist Commission
4th Fl., 630 Fifth Ave. 245-4000

6 Bahamas Tourist Office
Mezz. 52, 30 Rockefeller Plz. 757-1611

**11 Belgian American Chamber of
Commerce**
10th Fl., 50 Rockefeller Plz. 247-7613

11 Belgian Consulate
Rm. 1104, 50 Rockefeller Plz. 586-5110

12 Bermuda Department of Tourism
Rm. 646, 630 Fifth Ave. 397-7700

13 Bolivia, Republic of, Consulate
Rm. 620, 10 Rockefeller Plz. 586-1607

12 Brazilian Consulate
Rm. 2720, 630 Fifth Ave. 757-3080

3 Canadian Gov't. Office of Tourism
10th Fl., 1251 Ave. of Americas 757-4917

3 Canadian Consulate
16th Fl., 1251 Ave. of Americas 586-2400

12 Canadian National Railways
Mezz. 248, 630 Fifth Ave. 581-4318

12 Costa Rica Information Bureau
Rm. 242, 630 Fifth Ave. 245-6370

12 Costa Rica/LACSA Airlines
Rm. 242, 630 Fifth Ave. 245-6370.

8 Ecuador, Republic of, Consulate
Rm. 2411, 1270 Ave. of Americas 245-5380

14 Estonia, Republic of, Consulate
Rm. 1421, One Rockefeller Plz. 247-1450

12 Europe by Car
Rm. 280, 630 Fifth Ave. 581-3040

16 French National Railroads
Rm. 516, 610 Fifth Ave. 582-2110

12 Globetrotter of Scandinavia, tour service
Mezz. 226, 630 Fifth Ave. 582-0201

12 Grand Trunk Railway System
Mezz. 248, 630 Fifth Ave. 581-4318

12 Greyhound Group Charter Bus Service
Rm. 2650, 630 Fifth Ave. 245-7010

8 Haiti Gov't. Tourist Bureau
Rm. 508, 1270 Ave. of Americas 757-3517

12 Ibusz Hungarian Travel Bureau
Rm. 520, 630 Fifth Ave. 582-7412

12 Idemitsu Apollo, Japanese tours
Rm. 3101, 630 Fifth Ave. 757-4433

6 India Government Tourist Office
Mezz. 15, 30 Rockefeller Plz. 586-4901

12 Intercontinental Travel Systems, Inc.
Rm. 280, 630 Fifth Ave. 246-6885

12 Intourist—U.S.S.R.
Rm. 868, 630 Fifth Ave. 757-3884

12 Italian Government Travel Office
Rm. 1565, 630 Fifth Ave. 245-4822

12 Japan Travel Bureau International, Inc.
Rm. 550, 45 Rockefeller Plz. 246-8030

12 Japanese National Railways
Rm. 1961, 45 Rockefeller Plz. 757-9070

6 Kuwait Airways
Mezz. 20, 30 Rockefeller Plz. 581-9412

6 Lister International Travel Service, Inc.
Mezz. 12, 30 Rockefeller Plz. 582-3460

12 Malev Hungarian Airlines
Rm. 2602, 630 Fifth Ave. 757-6480

12 Misr Travel
Rm. 518, 630 Fifth Ave. 582-9210

6 Mon Voyage Travel, Inc.
Mezz. 21, 30 Rockefeller Plz. 586-8980

14 Netherlands Consulate
11th Fl., One Rockefeller Plz. 246-1429

14 Netherlands Chamber of Commerce
11th Fl., One Rockefeller Plz. 265-6460

12 New Zealand Consulate
Rm. 530, 630 Fifth Ave. 586-0060

12 New Zealand Travel Commissioner
Rm. 530, 630 Fifth Ave. 586-0060

3 Ontario, Gov't. of
Rm. 1080, 1251 Ave. of Americas 247-2744

1 Orient Holiday
1211 Ave. of Americas 221-6075

13 Peru, Republic of, consulate
Rm. 729, 10 Rockefeller Plz. 265-2480

12 Pisa Brothers, Inc., travel service
Rm. 2208, 630 Fifth Ave. 265-8420

12 Portuguese Consulate
Rm. 655, 630 Fifth Ave. 246-4580

12 Republic Airlines
Rm. 930, 630 Fifth Ave. 489-0784

**8 Robert Reid Associates, Inc., hotel
information**
Rm. 2418, 1270 Ave. of Americas 757-2444

6 Rockresorts, Inc., hotel information
Rm. 5400, 30 Rockefeller Plz. 586-4459

8 Room Center U.K. Inc.—British hotels
Rm. 2114, 1270 Ave. of Americas 246-7110

12 Royal Viking Lines
Rm. 1540, 630 Fifth Ave. 757-0921

12 Sea Sun Holidays
Rm. 863, 630 Fifth Ave. 765-0571

12 Solmar Chartering Services
Rm. 1400, 630 Fifth Ave. 765-3210

16 South African Tourist Corp.
Rm. 404, 610 Fifth Ave. 245-3720

14 Sun Line Agencies, steamship line
Rm. 315, 15 W. 48th St. 397-6400

12 Thai Airways International
Rm. 226, 630 Fifth Ave. 489-1634

6 Trafalgar Tours U.S.A., Inc.
Rm. 3315, 30 Rockefeller Plz. 586-1785

12 Travel Bureau, Inc.
Rm. 244, 630 Fifth Ave. 586-5454

12 TWA Travel Information
Mezz. 255, 630 Fifth Ave. 290-2121

8 Virgin Islands Gov't. Tourist Office
Mezz., 1270 Ave. of Americas 582-4520

12 Yugoslav National Tourist Organization
Mezz. 212, 630 Fifth Ave. 757-2801

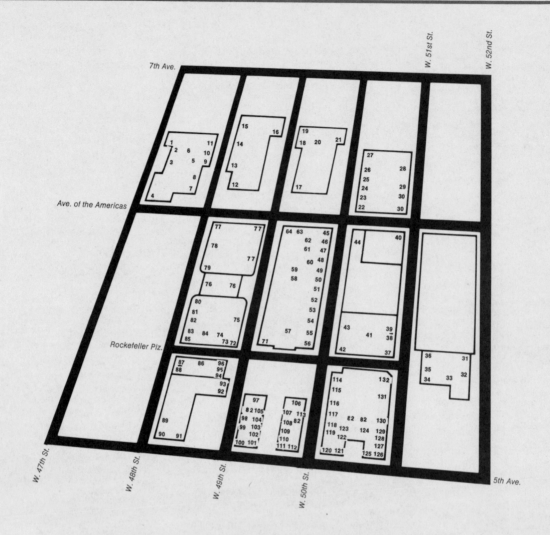

Banks

75 Banco de Ponce
10 Rockefeller Plz.   246-4900

72 Bank Hapoalim, B.M.
36 W. 49th St.   397-9650

22 Bank Of Tokyo Trust Co.
1271 Ave. of Americas   766-3198

132 Bankers Trust Co.
51 Rockefeller Plz.   957-9300

116 Barclays Bank of New York
15 W. 50th St.   265-1105

4   Chase Manhattan Bank
1211 Ave. of Americas   223-5741

71 Chase Manhattan Bank
30 Rockefeller Plz.   223-7966

34 Chemical Bank
11 W. 51st St.   922-5714

17 Chemical Bank
1251 Ave. of Americas   922-4156

35 Daiwa Bank Trust Company
75 Rockefeller Plz.   399-8500

114 East River Savings Bank
41 Rockefeller Plz.   553-9823

87 European American Bank & Trust Co.
19 W. 48th St.   437-4674

40 First Federal Savings & Loan Assoc.
1274 Ave. of Americas   397-9800

12 Irving Trust Co.
1221 Ave. of Americas   922-8295

56 Manufacturers Hanover Trust Co.
30 Rockefeller Plz.   974-1666

30 Manufacturers Hanover Trust Co.
1275 Ave. of Americas   974-1794

42 Morgan Guaranty Trust Co.
40 Rockefeller Plz.   483-2323

77 The New York Bank for Savings
1230 Ave. of Americas   841-6800

27 The Seaman's Bank for Savings
127 W. 50th St.   797-5000

37 Societe Generale
60 Rockefeller Plz.   397-6000

Entertainment

43 The Guild Theatre, films
33 W. 50th St.   757-2406

44 Radio City Music Hall Entertainment Center
1260 Ave. of Americas
box office—246-4600
information—757-3100

60 Rockefeller Center Guided Tours
30 Rockefeller Plz.   489-2947

Restaurants & Food Services

131 The Assembly Steak & Fish House
16 W. 51st St.   581-3580

32 The Bombay Palace,
Indian cuisine
30 W. 52nd St.   541-7777

36 The Brew Burger
21 W. 51st St.   563-7440

38 Center Coffee House
36 W. 51st St.   582-2280

85 Charley O's, Irish pub/chop house
33 W. 48th St.   582-7141

1 **Dish of Salt,** Chinese cuisine
133 W. 47th St. 921-4242

19 **Dosanko/Jinya Sushi,** Japanese cuisine
123 W. 49th St. 245-4090

15 **Fritzl's,** Swiss snack shop
129 W. 48th St. 575-1877

55 **Greentrees,** coffee shop
42 W. 50th St. 582-9025

64 **Hurley's,** steaks/seafood
1240 Ave. of Americas 765-8981

45 **Lindy's**
1250 Ave. of Americas 586-8986

61 **Pastrami 'N Things**
30 Rockefeller Plz. 247-4700

79 **Raga,** Indian cuisine
57 W. 48th St. 757-3450

31 **San Marco,** Italian cuisine
36 W. 52nd St. 246-5340

28 **U.S. Steakhouse**
120 W. 51st St. 757-8800

Shops & Services

13 **American Greetings Card Shop**
1221 Ave. of Americas 869-8780

41 **Antiquarian Booksellers Center**
50 Rockefeller Plz. 246-2564

50 **Bancroft,** men's apparel
54 W. 50th St. 489-1592

63 **Bancroft,** men's apparel
1250 Ave. of Americas 245-6821

80 **Bancroft,** men's apparel
45 W. 48th St. 586-2756

91 **Barnes & Noble Bookstore**
600 Fifth Ave. 765-0590

39 **Berlitz School of Languages/
Translation Service**
40 W. 51st St. 765-1000

93 **Books Kinokuniya,** Japanese book
sales
10 W. 49th St. 765-1461

101 **Botticelli,** shoes
612 Fifth Ave. 582-6313

24 **Cindy Shoes,** women's
115 W. 50th St. 489-4817

5 **The Complete Copy Center**
1211 Ave. of Americas 921-2050

98 **Continental Quilt Shoppe**
7 W. 49th St. 757-3511

68 **Courmettes & Gaul Opticians**
55 W. 49th St. 247-0988

23 **Cover-Ups,** women's apparel
113 W. 50th St. 581-3285

111 **Custom Shop**
618 Fifth Ave. 245-2499

54 **Cutler Owens,** sporting goods
44 W. 50th St. 582-7770

100 **Pierre d'Alby,** women's apparel
610 Fifth Ave. 541-7110

49 **Dan's Gifts,** souvenir shop
58 W. 50th St. 246-2771

6 **Datel Systems Corp.,** computers
1211 Ave. of Americas 921-0110

74 **David's Shirts,** custom shirts
10 Rockefeller Plz. 757-1083

124 **Deak-Perera Fifth Avenue, Inc.,**
money exchange
630 Fifth Ave. 757-6915

109 **Desiderio,** leather goods
620 Fifth Avenue 247-7625

69 **Dextor & Co., Inc.,** leather goods/gifts
53 W. 49th St. 245-7460

112 **Alfred Dunhill of London,** smoker's
supplies/gifts
620 Fifth Ave. 481-6950

47 **Fanny Farmer Candies**
62 W. 50th St. 581-9770

29 **Fifth Avenue Card Shop**
118 W. 51st St. 246-2539

20 **Film 'N Finish**
1251 Ave. of Americas 581-7996

65 **Foot-So-Port Shoe Shop**
63 W. 49th St. 582-0499

9 **G&G,** women's apparel
1211 Ave. of Americas 279-4961

76 **Garage,** Rockefeller Center
50 W. 49th St./49 W. 48th St. 489-5880

78 **Gruntal & Co.,** brokerage
61 W. 48th St. 581-9800

53 **Hoffritz for Cutlery**
46 W. 50th St. 757-3497

57 **Information Desk**
Lobby, 30 Rockefeller Plz. 489-2950

11 **Irene Hayes, Wadley & Smythe,** florist
1211 Ave. of Americas 869-0011

88 **Irene Hayes Wadley & Smythe,** florist
11 W. 48th St. 247-0051

8 **Jean Country,** jeans
1211 Ave. of Americas 354-8399

51 **Johnston & Murphy,** men's shoes
52 W. 50th St. 307-5061

10 **Labels for Less,** women's apparel
1211 Ave. of Americas 997-1032

103 **Librairie de France/Libreria Hispanica**
610 Fifth Ave. 581-8810

108 **Linea Garbo Shoes,** women's
620 Fifth Ave. 246-1938

82 **Lloyd & Haig,** men's shoes
37 W. 48th St. 974-0242

7 **London Majesty,** tall men's shop
1211 Ave. of Americas 221-1860

52 **Louis Martin Jewelers**
48 W. 50th St. 245-5566

104 **MacKeen Inc.,** sportswear
610 Fifth Ave. 977-9042

67 **Manfra, Tordella & Brookes,**
money exchange
59 W. 49th St. 974-3400

42 **N.C.R. Corporation,** wholesale
48 Rockefeller Plz. 484-5400

Newsstands
located in various building lobbies

106 **Nikon House,** product showroom
16 W. 50th St. 586-3907

66 **Pants And...,** sportswear
61 W. 49th St. 757-8550

62 **Party Bazaar,** cards/gifts
1250 Ave. of Americas 581-0310

58 **Photomart 49th Ltd.**
30 Rockefeller Plz. 582-4996

0 **Plymouth Shops,** women's apparel
1251 Ave. of Americas 873-5600

14 **Raemart Drugs**
111 W. 48th St. 575-0047

26 **Russell Stover Candies**
121 W. 50th St. 581-2177

70 **Senli Design Collection Ltd.,** gifts
51 W. 49th St. 582-1083

84 **Services Unlimited,** motor vehicle
bureau services
10 Rockefeller Plz. 586-8880

97 **Singer Sewing Center**
11 W. 49th St. 582-4473

113 **Arthur C. Sogno Co.,** jewelers
12 W. 50th St. 247-2980

16 **Strawberry,** women's apparel
120 W. 49th St. 391-8718

25 **Susan Michael's Fine Jewelers**
117 W. 50th St. 541-8951

110 **Teuscher Chocolates of Switzerland**
620 Fifth Ave. 246-4416

48 **Trapeze,** women's apparel
60 W. 50th St. 582-7068

81 **Wright Arch Preserver Shoe Shop,**
men's
39 W. 48th St. 265-3250

Travel

83 **A.N.A. Travel Advisers**
10 Rockefeller Plz. 581-0440

96 **Aerolinas Argentinas**
20 W. 49th St. 757-6400

129 **Aero Peru**
8 W. 51st St. 765-2200

123 **Air Panama**
630 Fifth Ave. 246-4033

95 **American Airlines**
18 W. 49th St. 661-4242

130 **AMTRAK**
12 W. 51st St. 736-4545

99 **BWIA International**
5 W. 49th St. 581-3200

107 **China Airlines**
620 Fifth Ave. 581-6500

46 **Dominicana Airlines**
64 W. 50th St. 397-3420

73 **Eastern Airlines**
10 Rockefeller Plz. 986-5000

122 **Egyptian Government Tourist Office**
630 Fifth Ave. 246-6960

105 **El Al Israel Airlines**
610 Fifth Ave. 486-2600

21 **Exxon Touring Service**
1251 Ave. of Americas 398-2690

121 **French Tourist Organization/French
West Indies Tourist Bureau**
628 Fifth Ave. 757-1125

102 **Icelandair**
610 Fifth Ave. 757-8585

2 **Iraqi Airways**
1211 Ave. of Americas 921-8990

118 **Japan National Tourist Organization**
11 W. 50th St. 757-5640

128 **Lan-Chile Airlines**
6 W. 51st St. 582-3250

90 **Pan American World Airways**
600 Fifth Ave. 973-4000

119 **Philippine Airlines**
7 W. 50th St. 247-2421

115 **Quebec Government Tourist Office**
17 W. 50th St. 397-0200

94 **Sabena — Belgian World Airways**
16 W. 49th St. 961-6200

126 **Scandinavian Airlines System**
638 Fifth Ave. 841-0102

120 **Trans World Airways**
624 Fifth Ave. 290-2121

125 **Varig Brazilian Airlines**
634 Fifth Ave. 340-0200

86 **Virginia State Travel Service**
11 Rockefeller Plz. 245-3080

127 **Yugoslav Airlines, JAT**
4 W. 51st St. 757-9676

Concourse Level Directory

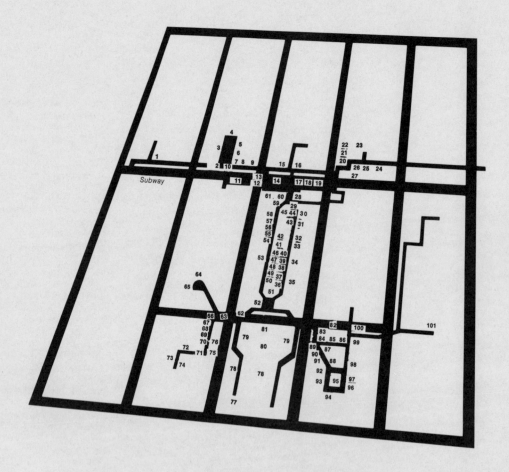

Banks

99 Bankers Trust
630 Fifth Ave. 957-9300

91 Barclays Bank of New York
630 Fifth Ave. 265-1105

16 Chemical Bank
1251 Ave. of Americas 922-4156

82 East River Savings Bank
41 Rockefeller Plz. 553-9823

28 First Federal Savings & Loan
Subway Mezz./50th St. 397-9800

35 Manufacturers Hanover Trust
30 Rockefeller Plz. 974-1666

24 Manufacturers Hanover Trust
1271 Ave. of Americas 974-1794

60 The New York Bank for Savings
Subway Mezz./50th St. 841-6800

Entertainment

4 The New York Experience Theater
1221 Ave. of Americas 869-0346

80 Rockefeller Center Outdoor Skating Rink
Lower Plaza
October through April 757-6230

Restaurants & Food Services

19 Barbara's, A Nice Little Place
Subway Mezz./50th St. 765-8122

2 **The Beanstalk**
1221 Ave. of Americas 354-4670

26 **Bonjour Coffee Shop**
1271 Ave. of Americas 265-3540

32 **Burger Train**
30 Rockefeller Plz. 586-0171

13 **The Cookie Station**
Subway Mezz./50th St. 246-3162

34 **The Crepe Place**
30 Rockefeller Plz. 246-5807

25 **Dawson's Pub**
1271 Ave. of Americas 265-3545

43 **Fro-gurt Shoppe**
30 Rockefeller Plz. 582-8092

68 **General Nutrition Center, health foods**
One Rockefeller Plz. 581-2787

14 **Grand Gourmet, take-out**
Subway Mezz./50th St. 541-5130

33 **Greengrocer's Pantry, take-out**
30 Rockefeller Plz. 586-0132

64 **Hamburger Center, U.S.A.**
10 Rockefeller Plz. 757-2455

96 **International Cafe**
630 Fifth Ave. 581-3580

27 **La Petite Brasserie**
1271 Ave. of Americas 265-3545

15 **Lamston's Cafeteria**
1251 Ave. of Americas 757-3430

18 **Little Nick Pizza**
Subway Mezz./50th St. 974-9310

17 **Nedick's**
Subway Mezz./50th St. 560-8036

76 **The Nook**
One Rockefeller Plz. 757-6575

98 **Old Times Restaurant & Bar**
630 Fifth Ave. 581-3626

44 **Pain Francais**
30 Rockefeller Plz. 541-8507

26 **Southampton Caterers**
1271 Ave. of Americas 265-3545

Shops & Services

1 **AM International**
1211 Ave. of Americas 840-5600

94 **Amal Printing**
630 Fifth Ave. 247-3270

50 **Anand India Shop**
30 Rockefeller Plz. 247-2054

36 **Belmont Bird & Kennel Shop**
30 Rockefeller Plz. 247-0620

42 **Benjamin Book**
30 Rockefeller Plz. 586-8911

49 **Burton-Page Galleries**
30 Rockefeller Plz. 307-5310

90 **B.G. Canevares Jewelers**
630 Fifth Ave. 247-5644

3 **Cardio Fitness Center**
1221 Ave. of Americas 840-8240

5 **Casella Pen & Souvenir Shop**
1221 Ave. of Americas 869-9492

23 **Joseph Cione Haircutters**
1271 Ave. of Americas 586-7995

22 **The Complete Copy Center**
1271 Ave. of Americas 757-7303

71 **Computer Pictures Corp.**
600 Fifth Ave. 307-6108

7 **Concourse Tobacconist**
1221 Ave. of Americas 869-8988

101 **Cosmos Ticket Office**
75 Rockefeller Plz. 265-8600

38 **Fanny Farmer Candies**
30 Rockefeller Plz. 581-9770

45 **Federal Express**
30 Rockefeller Plz.

58 **Dr. Ronald Fields, optometrist**
30 Rockefeller Plz. 247-7392

61 **Fotomat**
Subway Mezz./50th St. 541-5140

9 **General Shoe Repair**
1221 Ave. of Americas 869-3552

11 **General Shoe Repair**
Subway Mezz./50th St. 869-3552

97 **General Shoe Repair**
630 Fifth Ave. 869-3552

66 **Haircutting by Jason**
10 Rockefeller Plz. 489-3232

12 **Harris Florist**
Subway Mezz./50th St. 246-6640

39 **Hellenic Arts Crystal & Glass**
30 Rockefeller Plz. 246-3570

73 **Irene Hermann Lettershop**
600 Fifth Ave. 247-6671

89 **International Flower Shop**
630 Fifth Ave. 265-2878

100 **ITT World Communications, telegrams**
50 Rockefeller Plz. 797-7530

83 **Karann Boutique Ltd., handbags**
630 Fifth Ave. 765-8161

15 **Lamston's, variety store**
1251 Ave. of Americas 757-3430

77 **Librairie de France/Libreria Hispanica**
610 Fifth Ave. 581-8810

65 **Lloyds Messenger Service**
10 Rockefeller Plz. 586-5090

55 **Dr. Barry S. Marquit, podiatrist**
30 Rockefeller Plz. 246-3364

86 **Marvel Cleaners**
630 Fifth Ave. 247-1522

30 **Marvel Cleaners**
30 Rockefeller Plz. 245-5343

10 **McGraw-Hill Bookstore**
1221 Ave. of Americas 997-4100

8 **B. Nelson Custom Shoes**
1221 Ave. of Americas 869-3552

Newsstands
located in various Concourse areas

51 **Party Bazaar, cards/gifts**
30 Rockefeller Plz. 581-0310

95 **Passport Acme Photo**
630 Fifth Ave. 247-2911

93 **Penn Office Supply**
630 Fifth Ave. 246-6022

63 **Perfection Graphics**
One Rockefeller Plz. 541-9060

21 **Photomart 50th Ltd.**
1271 Ave. of Americas 265-4245

52 **Plaza Jewelry and Gifts**
30 Rockefeller Plz. 265-3137

20 **Plymouth Shops, women's apparel**
1271 Ave. of Americas 873-5600

31 **Plymouth Shops, women's accessories**
30 Rockefeller Plz. 245-9741

40 **Plymouth Shops, women's apparel**
30 Rockefeller Plz. 245-9741

47 **Plymouth Shops, women's apparel**
30 Rockefeller Plz. 245-9741

87 **Plymouth Shops, women's apparel**
630 Fifth Ave. 245-9741

92 **Quick Service Messenger Co.**
630 Fifth Ave. 725-0500

56 **RMH International, gifts**
30 Rockefeller Plz. 757-5535

53 **Raemart Drugs**
30 Rockefeller Plz. 757-9335

59 **Ruth Hats and Handbags**
30 Rockefeller Plz. 245-8924

74 **Bernard Samter, watch repair**
600 Fifth Ave. 757-2633

46 **Seki Jewelers**
30 Rockefeller Plz. 582-3893

48 **Soeda Gift Shop**
30 Rockefeller Plz. 265-7731

69 **Stampvest International, philatelic services**
One Rockefeller Plz. 765-2058

54 **Step 'N Style Shoes**
30 Rockefeller Plz. 757-6690

75 **Tobron Office Furniture**
One Rockefeller Plz. 245-5656

78 **U.S. Post Office**
610 Fifth Ave. 265-3854

88 **Jerry Vukic's Men's Hair Salon**
630 Fifth Ave. 246-3151

Travel

85 **Harmal Travel Service**
630 Fifth Ave. 581-3634

84 **New England Vacation Center**
630 Fifth Ave. 307-5780

6 **Ritter Travel Bureau**
1221 Ave. of Americas 869-3555

72 **Travelroutes International**
600 Fifth Ave. 765-9778

Chronology of Key Events

Prior to 1801
The site of Rockefeller Center was pasture land owned by the City of New York. It consisted of most of the three blocks today bounded by 48th and 51st Sts., and Fifth Avenue and the Avenue of the Americas.

1801
Property acquired by Dr. David Hosack, eminent physician, botanist, and teacher. Dr. Hosack constructed the Elgin Botanic Garden for use in teaching medical students about plants used in treating disease.

1811
Dr. Hosack sold the land to the State of New York, the gardens being too costly for him to maintain. Gardens came under supervision of the Regents of the State of New York, who assigned management to the College of Physicians and Surgeons, Columbia University.

1814
Columbia University gained ownership of the land in an aid-to-education act. Columbia University was expected to move its campus from lower Manhattan within twelve years under terms of the act.

1819
Legislature relieved Columbia of the requirement to move and Columbia leased the gardens to a succession of tenants.

1852
Columbia rented the property in small lots. It had been divided earlier into more than 250 lots for one-family dwellings.

1926
Metropolitan Opera Company considered the Columbia property as a possible site for new opera house. John D. Rockefeller, Jr., spearheaded the drive for new opera house and began negotiations with Columbia for the land.

1928
Metropolitan Square Corporation organized to handle opera house project which consisted of a site for the new opera house and plans to sublease land to commercial interests who would erect their own buildings.

October 1, 1928
Mr. Rockefeller and Columbia reached an agreement on land assignment rights.

January 22, 1929
Land officially leased from Columbia.

October 1, 1929
John R. Todd signed agreement making his company, Todd, Robertson & Todd Engineering Corporation, manager of the project.

October 22, 1929
Reinhard (L. Andrew Reinhard) & Hofmeister (Henry Hofmeister) retained as the general architects of Rockefeller Center. Todd also employed Raymond Hood, of Hood & Fouilhoux, and Harvey Wiley Corbett, of Corbett, Harrison & MacMurray, as architectural consultants. (Wallace K. Harrison later became a primary architect of the project.) These architects and others involved in this "architecture by committee" became known as the "Associated Architects."

December 6, 1929
Metropolitan Opera Company abandoned the project because of legal problems and onset of Depression.

May 17, 1930
Actual work began on clearing the property, mainly occupied by five-story brownstone buildings, small shops, and speakeasies.

July 26, 1931
Eight steam shovels, 100 trucks and between 200 and 300 men began excavation of 60 percent of total area of three blocks. (Foundations for RKO, Radio City Music Hall, RCA and RCA West, Center Theater.) Debris taken to old South Reservoir in Central Park which was filled in for a playground.

July 30, 1931
Contract (considered at that time the world's largest) signed with Pittsburgh Plate Glass Company for glass to be used in 12,320 windows and 17,600 doors. About 1,000,000 sq. ft. which, if spread flat, would cover 23 acres.

August 17, 1931
Contract (considered at that time the world's largest) signed with Anaconda Wire and Cable Company for 7,800,000 feet of wire and cable. Total individual strands joined together would extend over 15,000 miles. Contract signed with American Brass Company for all major brass and copper products other than cable or wire; pipe alone would extend 200 miles.

August 25, 1931
Contract (considered at that time the world's largest) for 20,000 cast-iron radiators, approximately 660,000 sq. ft. of radiation surface.

September 18, 1931
Final acquisition of all land and leases necessary to building of Rockefeller Center. Three hundred eighty-three legal documents filed in Register's office in City Hall consisting of various instruments by which the interests of tenants and sub-tenants were taken over. Over two years' work and several million dollars spent in obtaining leases. There had been 229 buildings on property; on this date only 59 were still standing and about 25 percent were vacant. (First of 383 leases was purchased in February 1929.)

November 1931
Construction started on Radio City Music Hall.

Christmas Eve, 1931
The celebration of Christmas in Rockefeller Center started informally when a small tree was placed on the site of the British Empire Building and La Maison Française soon after demolition of brownstones in that area had been completed. It was decorated with tinsel and gaily colored ornaments. An early photo shows workmen lined up around the tree to receive their pay on Christmas Eve.

January 1932
Construction started on RCA, RCA West, and Center Theater (now the site of the Simon & Schuster Building, 1230 Avenue of the Americas).

January 7, 1932
Announcement of British Empire Building under sponsorship of important British interests headed by Lord Southborough.

March 15, 1932
Contract for mural awarded Ezra Winter for Grand Foyer of Music Hall — first in long series of contracts for decorative program.

April 27, 1932
Name of Metropolitan Square Corporation, holding company, changed to Rockefeller Center, Inc., thus severing last tie with original plan in connection with Metropolitan Opera Association.

May 2, 1932
Lease between Rockefeller Center, Inc., RCA, and NBC, and announcement of name, "RCA Building."

May 24, 1932
Senator Robert F. Wagner introduced "Exhibition Act" bill into U.S. Senate, which permitted foreign firms in Rockefeller Center to bring in goods duty-free for display purposes.

July 20, 1932
President Hoover signed "Exhibition Act" bill.

September 26, 1932
Topping-out ceremony on RCA Building at 3 P.M. with unfurling of American flag on north side of structure. Fifty-three old dwellings and stores yielded 31,000 truckloads of debris: 170,000 cubic yards of earth and rock, weighing more than 250,000 tons. New construction used approximately 60,000 tons of steel, with heaviest columns weighing 60 tons each; 6,000 aluminum spandrels; and 212,000 cubic feet of limestone.

October 10, 1932
Announcement that Frank Brangwyn, Diego

Rivera, and José María Sert awarded contracts for RCA Building murals.

November 25, 1932
Air-conditioning contract (considered at that time to be one of the largest awarded) went to Carrier Engineering Corporation. Involved over a million dollars and provided equipment capable of refrigeration equal to 3 million pounds of melting ice a day.

December 1932
Opening of RKO Building, Music Hall, and Center Theater.

January 30, 1933
Contract for statue of Prometheus awarded to Paul Manship.

May 1933
RCA Building opened.

February 27, 1934
First in a long line of exhibitions opened by Mayor LaGuardia — "First Municipal Art Exhibition"—in space later occupied by Museum of Science & Industry in the RCA Building.

October 3, 1934
Rainbow Room formally opened.

June 17, 1936
Promenade Cafe opened.

December 9, 1936
Construction started on Rockefeller Plaza Skating Pond.

December 25, 1936
Skating Pond opened.

March/April 1939
Demolition of Sixth Avenue "El."

Spring 1939
First Easter Lily display, which has become an annual tradition, in the Channel Gardens.

November 1, 1939
"Last Rivet Ceremony" celebrated completion of U.S. Rubber Building (now the Simon & Schuster Building), at the time thought to be the last building of Rockefeller Center. John D. Rockefeller, Jr., drove the last rivet into the building.

1947
Prometheus regilded for the first time since its installation in 1934.

1951
Air-conditioning program, lasting until 1958, undertaken in older structures of Center to bring systems up-to-date.

May 1957
Rockefeller Center expanded for first time to west side of Avenue of the Americas, when excavation started for new Time & Life Building at 1271 Avenue of the Americas.

July 2, 1957
Sidewalk Superintendents Club, Time & Life Chapter, opened, with Marilyn Monroe present at ceremonies. Within three months, a quarter-of-a-million sidewalk superintendents from 51 countries had signed the Club's register.

December 26, 1957
Rockefeller Center signed lease with Transit Authority for northern mezzanine of IND Subway Station at 50th Street and Avenue of the Americas; RCI renovated area into clean and attractive shop area, comparable to rest of concourse, and maintains it.

1958
Prometheus regilded a second time.

May 27, 1958
Fountain of Lights, installed behind Prometheus to form a backdrop curtain of water with light display turned on.

December 1959
Time & Life Building opened.

January 13, 1961
Rockefeller Center joined in Sperry Building project (1290 Avenue of the Americas). Rock-Uris partnership formed with development firm of Webb & Knapp and Uris Buildings Corporation.

February 24, 1961
Rock-Hil-Uris Corporation (including the Hilton Hotel chain) formed to erect hotel two blocks to the northwest of 1290 Avenue of the Americas.

March 25, 1961
Excavation started for Hilton Hotel.

November 1962
Sperry Rand Building opened.

May 15, 1963
Sinclair Oil Building (600 Fifth Avenue) added to the Center.

1963
Prometheus regilded a third time.

June 26, 1963
New York Hilton opened.

August 1968
Excavation started for Exxon Building, 1251 Avenue of the Americas.

December 1968
Excavation started for McGraw-Hill Building, 1221 Avenue of the Americas.

June 1969
The American Institute of Architects selected Rockefeller Center to receive its first 25-Year Award.

July 1969
Hilton Hotels Corporation purchased Rockefeller Center's interests in Rock-Hil-Uris, Inc.

September 1970
Excavation started for Celanese Building, 1211 Avenue of the Americas.

September 1971
Exxon Building opened.

March 1972
McGraw-Hill Building opened.

Spring 1973
Celanese Building opened.

1976
Program begun to clean façade of 14 original buildings of the Center. Believed to be one of the largest building cleaning programs ever undertaken.
Rockefeller Center cited by the American Institute of Architects as second among 260 nominations for most significant architectural achievement in the nation's first 200 years. First place was awarded Thomas Jefferson's design for the University of Virginia.

March 1978
Radio City Music Hall designated an interior landmark by New York City Landmarks Preservation Commission.

February 1979
Radio City Music Hall Productions, Inc., national entertainment production company, formed. Radio City Music Hall interior fully restored by Rockefeller Center, Inc.

1980
Limestone façade of RCA Building washed in two-stage water process to restore it to its original luster. This completed program to clean façade of all Center's original buildings.

Personalities and Comments

John D. Rockefeller, Jr.

"We were perfectly thrilled with the theatre. Perhaps you will remember that when I first saw the model of its interior in the architects' office I said I did not know what style it was, whether modern or adapted from the past, but that I liked it tremendously. That same feeling was upon me, only enhanced tenfold, as I saw the realization of the structure of which the model was prophetic. I think the great auditorium is beautiful, soul-satisfying and inspiring beyond anything I dreamed possible. It is really a great achievement. I liked it in every detail, the gayly upholstered seats with their black edge and black arms and the charming two-toned black carpet included. The lobby is as distinguished and unusual and truly impressive as the theatre itself. Words fail me with which to express adequately my delight with the Ezra Winters painting. I can imagine nothing that could be more beautiful, more decorative and more completely satisfying in that location. Whether one looks directly at the painting or sees some portion of it reflected in the myriad of mirrors, the effect is always charming and beautiful. I liked too the great simplicity of the wall spaces with their long, brilliant mirrors flanked by the sombre velvet panels. We visited the various galleries and withdrawing rooms on each floor. These rooms are all of them interesting, unusual and distinguished to an extraordinary degree. There is a style and chic about the whole building which is impressive in the extreme.

"You and your associates, architects and builders, have sometimes thought me critical and exacting. So much the more welcome, therefore, I trust, will be these unqualified expressions of my profound appreciation of this last creation of your united efforts—a creation which is a real triumph, an achievement of which you may always be justly proud."

—Letter from JDR, Jr. to John R. Todd
November 10, 1932

"Perhaps the most important elimination from our theaters, which forms its most outstanding item of progress, is the over-hanging balcony. For years I have studied the reactions of crowds in balconies, and long ago decided that the balcony is not ideal for the group contact so vital in the theater. There is mass thought, emotion and confidence when a crowd is in a huddle...In a huge balcony this is impossible."

—Roxy Rothafel
Variety, December 20, 1932

"We work...from the inside out, first to get good plans for what we had to have and then to clothe those plans, as simply and attractively as possible, with clean-looking exteriors. We didn't want men ...too much committed to the architectural past or who were too much interested in wild modernism."

—John R. Todd

"We hope to impress the customers by sheer elegance, not by overwhelming them with ornament."
—Donald Deskey
August 1932

"While the prime consideration in this enterprise must be its financial success, the importance of a unified and beautiful architectural whole must be constantly kept in mind, and attained, to the fullest extent possible compatible with an adequate return on the investment."
—John D. Rockefeller, Jr.
memorandum, August 28, 1929.

"The International Music Hall will be a distinct departure from the dry, formal, academic treatment of the past. It will substitute for the gaudy gilt-ridden interiors of most theaters, a tasteful modern atmosphere. It will neither admit of dry imitation of traditional periods, nor its flouncy adaptation. This great entertainment hall will be completely and uncompromisingly contemporary in effect, as modern in its design of furniture, wallpapers, and murals as it will be in technical devices for stage presentations."
—Donald Deskey

"The architect is not one man; the design is the result of many minds working on the same problem from many angles. The results will be attributable to the group, to the "guild of master builders," if you will. All are architects in the sense that all contribute to the creation and the modification of the final result."
—L. Andrew Reinhard
Architectural Forum, 1932

"...though the New Yorker lives cheek by jowl with so many buildings ranked with the wonders of the world, we have seen that the average resident of a City, so especially privileged in buildings worth staring at, rarely looks at the outside of any building....In the normal course of his daily round the first thing—outside of his public traffic lane—that he sees is the lobby where he waits for his elevator. That is why so much attention is devoted to dolling up our lobbies and providing fancy cabs for the tenant to be shot upstairs in. But what the tenant really lives with during the long day...is the inside of his own office.

...the lobby of the building has all the latest approved effects: shining chromium plate overlaid on marble of curious colors: [but] even though it is lined with steel painted like an automobile—Mr. Jones on the 19th or Mr. Brown on the 30th may elect to surround himself with a complete Georgian setting.... He may enjoy during business hours a condition of insulation from the hectic City tempo almost complete as that achieved out there at his well appointed country place...

It is strictly true, however, that in cities the outside (which has always been less important really, than the inside) grows progressively less important still as it becomes more and more difficult for anybody—especially anybody who uses the building—to get the benefit of any kick there may be in standing off and looking at it. Possibly we may come (in time) to treating all city outsides like a tent—the Big Top for example, under which all subways run and the railways arrive—and having all the shows inside."
—Raymond Hood, "Hanging Gardens of New York"
T Square Club Journal, September 1931

Raymond Hood

Portfolio: The Center in Postcards

Postcards—or "postals" as they were once known—have been popular for nearly one hundred years as a way of showing the folks at home that you got around. In the thirties and forties cityscapes provided by Rockefeller Center made perfect postcard subjects: There was the serene beauty of the Gardens of Many Nations, the aerial views of the Center in which the skyscrapers seemed to soar above the surrounding streets, and, of course, the high-stepping, splendiferous Rockettes.

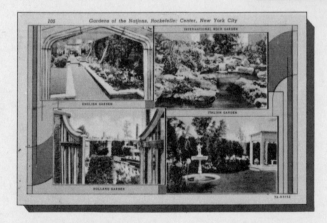

AIRPLANE VIEW OF ROCKEFELLER CENTER NEW YORK

INDEX

Illustration references are indicated by page numbers in *italics*.

Acknowledgments

The editors gratefully recognize the assistance of the managers and staff of Rockefeller Center, Inc. and Radio City Music Hall in the preparation of this book. In particular we would like to thank Erilyn Riley, Bevin Sloan, George Le Moine, Jaime Ramos and Barbara Singer for their generous cooperation. Finally, the author would like to express his appreciation for the assistance given him by Rockefeller Center, Inc.'s architectural consultant, Alexander Cooper.

Russell Bourne: *Editor*
Angelica Design Group, Ltd.: *Design*
Esther Brumberg: *Picture Editor*
Jeffrey Simpson: *Additional Text*
Ruth Malin: *Text Editor*
Barbara M. Strauch: *Project Manager*
Linda H. Alexander: *Editorial Assistant*

*Isamu Noguchi's dynamic,
10-ton stainless steel statue on
the Associated Press Building
represents "News."*